KOREAN WAR

IMJIN RIVER

FALL OF THE GLOSTERS TO THE ARMISTICE
APRIL 1951–JULY 1953

GERRY VAN TONDER

Pen & Sword

MILITARY

AN IMPRINT OF PEN & SWORD BOOKS LTD.
YORKSHIRE – PHILADELPHIA

First published in Great Britain in 2020 and reprinted in 2021 by
PEN AND SWORD MILITARY
an imprint of
Pen and Sword Books Ltd
47 Church Street
Barnsley
South Yorkshire S70 2AS

ISBN 978 1 52677 813 0

Typeset by Aura Technology and Software Services, India
Printed and bound in the UK by CPI Group (UK) Ltd, Croydon, CRO 4YY

Pen & Sword Books Ltd incorporates the imprints of Pen & Sword
Archaeology, Atlas, Aviation, Battleground, Discovery, Family History, History, Maritime, Military,
Naval, Politics, Railways, Select, Social History, Transport, True Crime, Claymore Press, Frontline
Books, Leo Cooper, Praetorian Press, Remember When, Seaforth Publishing and Wharncliffe.

For a complete list of Pen and Sword titles please contact
Pen and Sword Books Limited
47 Church Street, Barnsley, South Yorkshire, S70 2AS, England
email: enquiries@pen-and-sword.co.uk
website: www.pen-and-sword.co.uk

or
Pen and Sword Books
1950 Lawrence Rd, Havertown, PA 19083, USA
email: uspen-and-sword@casematepublishers.com
www.penandswordbooks.com

CONTENTS

GLOSSARY

CCP	Chinese Communist Party
CIA	Central Intelligence Agency (US)
CPVA	Chinese People's Volunteer Army
DPRK	Democratic People's Republic of Korea (North Korea)
EUSAK	Eighth United States Army in Korea
FAB	field artillery battalion
FEAF	Far East Air Forces (US)
GIAP	Guards Interceptor Air Regiment (Soviet)
HE	high explosive
HVAR	high-velocity aircraft rocket
IAD	Interceptor–fighter Air Division (Soviet)
IAK	Fighter Air Corps (Soviet)
IAP	Interceptor–fighter Air Regiment
JOC	Joint Operations Centre
JCS	Joint Chiefs of Staff (US)
KATUSA	Korean Augmentation to the US Army
KPA	Korean People's Army (North Korean)
MLR	main line of resistance
MSR	main supply route
PLA	People's Liberation Army (China)
PLAAF	People's Liberation Army Air Force (China)
PRC	People's Republic of China
RCT	Regimental Combat Team
ROK	Republic of Korea (South Korea)
ROKA	Republic of Korea Army (South Korean)
TF	task force
UNC	United Nations Command
USMC	United States Marine Corps

It will be noticed that many Korean names of places and geographical features either carry the same suffix or end in the same few letters. These define what a name is being applied to, e.g. Ch'ŏng*ch'ŏn* would be Ch'ŏng River: *ch'ŏn* or *gang* river; *do* island; *dong* town or village within a district or *ri*; *ni* town; *ri* town and surrounding district; *san* mountain. A CPVA army unit is the equivalent of a Western military corps, so for comparative purposes, the author has used the term corps.

TIMELINE

1910
Korea is annexed to the Japanese Empire.

1945
15 August: Japan surrenders. US President Harry S. Truman issues a General Order partitioning Korea at the 38th Parallel to facilitate Soviet and American occupying forces to disarm and demobilize the Japanese.
24 August: Soviet troops complete the occupation of their northern half of Korea.
8 September: US occupation forces arrive in Korea.

1947
14 November: The United Nations establishes the UN Temporary Commission on Korea (UNTCOK) for the sole purpose of supervising a general election throughout Korea.

1948
12 January: UNTCOK establishes its headquarters in the Seoul.
23 January: Soviet occupation forces block United Nations Commission on Korea (UNCOK) from entering North Korea.
10 May: UNTCOK supervises a general election held in South Korea.
15 August: An elected government of the Republic of Korea is formed.
12 December: The UN General Assembly recognizes the government of the Republic of Korea as the only lawful government in Korea. The permanent UN Commission on Korea is activated.
26 December: Soviet troops complete their withdrawal from North Korea.

1949
The US, Britain, Canada, New Zealand and Australia recognize the Republic of Korea.
29 June: American occupation forces complete their evacuation of South Korea.

1950
25 June: Massed Soviet-trained and -equipped North Korean forces invade the South.
26 June: The UN Security Council condemns the North Korean attack as a threat to regional peace and international security, calling on P'yŏngyang to withdraw back north of the 38th Parallel.
27 June: The UN Security Council calls upon all its member states to support South Korea. US President Harry S. Truman orders air and naval forces to support the South.

28 June: The South Korean government vacates the capital, Seoul.

29 June: Elements of the Royal Navy and the Royal Australian Navy arrive in Korean waters.

1 July: The UN creates a unified command and General Douglas MacArthur is appointed Commander-in-Chief.

14 July: South Korean forces are placed under the UN command.

20 July: Taejon falls to the North Koreans.

21 July: Canadian transport aircraft arrive in Korea.

30 July: Royal Canadian Navy forces arrive in Korean waters. The Naktong River defence line is established.

1 August: Royal New Zealand ships arrive in Korean waters.

28 August: The British 27th Infantry Brigade under Brigadier Basil A. Coad arrives at Pusan.

15 September: US-led UN forces launch an amphibious landing at Inch'ŏn.

16 September: UN forces commence a breakout from the defensive Pusan Perimeter.

28 September: UN forces liberate Seoul. The Royal Australian Regiment arrives in Korea.

1 October: South Korean forces cross the 38th Parallel into North Korea.

2 October: China threatens to intervene if UN forces enter North Korea.

7 October: The UN authorizes UN forces to pursue the retreating North Korean army into North Korea.

16 October: The Chinese People's Volunteer Army moved invades North Korea from Manchuria.

19 October: P'yŏngyang, capital of North Korea, is taken by UN forces.

26 October: UN forces reach the Yalu River border with China, where Chinese forces are engaged. US forces land at Wŏnsan on the Korean east coast.

27 October: The Chinese launch their first offensive against UN forces.

1 November: Chinese MiG fighter aircraft cross the Yalu River for the first time.

3–18 November: The British 29th (Independent) Brigade under Brigadier Thomas Brodie arrives at Pusan.

7 November: The Canadian 25th Infantry Brigade starts arriving at Pusan.

20 November: The 60th Indian Field Ambulance arrives in Korea.

24 November: General MacArthur orders his troops to march on the Yalu River.

25 November: The Chinese launch their second offensive.

27 November: Chinese troops penetrate the US Eighth Army line, cutting off the US 1st Marine Division at the Changjin (Chosin) Reservoir.

15 December: UN forces withdraw from Hŭngnam and Wŏnsan to consolidate on the 38th Parallel.

23 December: US Eighth Army commander, Lieutenant General Walton Walker is killed in a vehicle collision. He is succeeded by Lieutenant General Matthew B. Ridgway.

31 December: New Zealand field artillery arrives in South Korea.

1951

4 January: UN forces evacuate Seoul.

15 March: UN forces retake Seoul.

31 March: UN forces arrive at the 38th Parallel.

11 April: President Truman relieves General MacArthur of his command, replacing him with General Ridgway. General Van Fleet replaces Ridgway as commander of the US Eighth Army.

22 April: The CPVA launches its fifth 'spring' offensive, resulting in the battles of the Imjin River (Solma-ri) and Kap'yŏng.

16–18 May: Battle of Bunker Hill.

31 May: The US Fifth Air Force launches Operation Strangle to destroy the CPVA logistics infrastructure in northern South Korea.

1–12 June: The US Eighth Army executes Operation Piledriver to move onto Line Wyoming and secure the Iron Triangle.

25 June: Beijing supports the Soviet Union call for a ceasefire.

10 July: Armistice talks commence at Kaesŏng.

22 August: The Communist Chinese suspend the Kaesŏng talks.

13 September–15 October: UN forces fight costly battles at Bloody Ridge and Heartbreak Ridge.

28 September: Chairman of the US Joint Chiefs of Staff (JCS), General Omar N. Bradley, and Department of State counsellor Charles E. Bohlen visit Korea on a mission to reactivate the stalled armistice talks.

3 October: Lieutenant General John W. 'Iron Mike' O'Daniel, commander of the US I Corps, launches Operation Commando to move defensive positions near Yŏngch'ŏn 6 miles from Line Wyoming to Line Jamestown.

18 October: The US FEAF triggers the battle of Namsi to destroy airfields in north-west Korea.

25 October: Ceasefire talks resume at P'anmunjŏm.

12 November: General Ridgway orders a cessation of offensive operations, employing an 'active defence' strategy instead.

2 December: The four-month Operation Ratkiller is activated to neutralize guerrilla activity in south-western Korea.

1952

1 January: UN forces begin air and artillery attacks on CPVA and North Korean army (KPA) positions.

10–15 February: Attempts to lure CPVA and KPA troops into UN ambushes fail.

25 February: The US Fifth Air Force commences Operation Saturate, an aerial interdiction campaign aimed at CPVA road and rail bottlenecks.

12 May: Lieutenant General Mark Clark takes over from General Ridgway as commander of US Far East and commander of UN forces in Korea.

6 June: Strategically important hill feature 'Old Baldy' (Hill 275), south of the Yŏkgok-ch'ŏn River, is captured by the US 45th Division.

23 June: The USAF conducts bombing raids on power plants along the Yalu River.

29 August: P'yŏngyang is virtually destroyed in the largest American bombing raid of the war.

17–24 September: Elements of the US 65th Division suffer 10 per cent casualties in the battle for Kelly Hill.

6–15 October: UN and CPVA forces fight for control of Whitehorse Hill (Hill 395) commanding the Yŏkgok-ch'ŏn River near Ch'ŏrwŏn.

13 October–8 November: UN forces conduct limited offensive operations to capture strategic hills in the Iron Triangle.

14 October–5 November: The battle for Triangle Hill (Hill 598) takes place just north of Kimhwa.

24 October: Dwight D. Eisenhower succeeds Truman as president of the United States.

26 October–27 July 1953: A series of battles takes place on the Nevada Hill Complex that commands the Sami-ch'ŏn Valley approaches to Seoul.

2 November: US President Eisenhower embarks on a four-day visit to Korea.

1953

25 January: An ill-conceived air, armour and artillery attack by the US 7th Division—Operation Smack—on central CPVA positions fails, to the embarrassment of the United States.

10 February: Lieutenant General Maxwell Taylor replaces General Van Fleet as US Eighth Army commander.

5 March: Soviet Union premier Joseph Stalin dies.

23 March–11 July: A number of small but fierce clashes take place for control of Pork Chop Hill (Hill 234) near the 38th Parallel in western Korea.

20 April–3 May: In Operation Little Switch, there is an exchange of wounded and sick POWs between the warring sides.

10 May: The US FEAF commences a campaign of bombing raids on North Korean hydro-electric and irrigation reservoirs.

28 May: The Chinese commence their summer offensive by attacking US 25th Division outposts.

10–18 June: CPVA conducts several attacks on the US 3rd Division-held Outpost Harry, north-west of Kimhwa. The Chinese push the ROKA II Corps back 4,000 yards.

15–30 June: The US I Corps comes under sustained CPVA attacks.

18 June: South Korean President Syngman Rhee orders the release of North Korean POWs.

July: The US Navy's Task Force 77 is armed with nuclear weapons.

11 July: UN forces abandon Pork Chop Hill.

27 July: Leaders of all protagonists in the Korean War sign an agreement for the cessation of all hostilities, pending a final settlement.

INTRODUCTION

With the ultimate conquest of Nazi Germany in Europe and the capitulation of Imperial Japan in the Far East bringing the Second World War to an end, the victorious 'Big Powers' redefined their global interests. While the Soviet Union's Joseph Stalin firmly placed the Red flag over eastern Europe, President Harry S. Truman turned the occupied Japanese islands into a forward American stronghold of air, ground and naval forces facing the Soviet Union and China.

There would, however, be a divergence of strategic interest in the Korean peninsula which, for decades, had essentially been a Japanese foreign territory. Together with the Soviet Union, the Americans went through the motions of fulfilling a Potsdam obligation to act as caretakers pending the holding of elections in Korea. An arbitrary line thought up in a Washington back office—the 38th Parallel—delineated American and Soviet areas of transient responsibility on the peninsula: North and South Korea.

As it transpired, North Korea refused to participate in the May 1948 general elections, that saw South Korean Syngman Rhee become president of South Korea. The United Nations recognized the legitimacy of the post-war government, and by June 1949 the Americans and Russians had terminated their military presence on the peninsula. Four months later, Chairman Mao Zedong proclaimed the communist People's Republic of China.

To the south of the 38th Parallel, the Americans had no concern for the future security of their erstwhile wards, leaving the South Koreans militarily destitute. For the North, Stalin's agenda for the peninsula could not have been more different. Moscow selected, groomed, indoctrinated, and trained and equipped North Korean leader Kim Il-sung and his army. Towards the end of the Second World War in the Far East, Soviet forces had cleared Chinese Manchuria of the Japanese before handing the territory, on North Korea's border, over to the Chinese communists. Stalin then sat back, having significantly created a vast swathe of red to the south of his nation.

In the first of six volumes on the Korean War, the author describes how

North Korea launches a massive attack on the south, crossing the 38th Parallel in west to east phases. In Washington and Tokyo, the Americans were caught totally by surprise, with most enjoying a leisurely weekend away from the office. Ill-prepared and poorly equipped, South Korean forces and the US troops thrown in to execute holding-only positions suffered humiliating defeat after defeat as the North Koreans swept down the peninsula, in an invasion reminiscent of Hitler's blitzkrieg across a helpless Western Europe.[*]

---

[*] Gerry van Tonder, *North Korea Invades the South: Across the 38th Parallel, June 1950* (Pen and Sword Military, Barnsley, 2018).

Caught totally by surprise, both Washington and the US Far East Command in Japan had no contingency to systematically deal with the unexpected crisis in Korea when North Korean ground forces, armour and artillery crossed the 38th Parallel on 25 June 1950. The South Korean capital, Seoul, fell three days later.

As the Korean People's Army (KPA) 2nd, 3rd and 6th divisions pushed down the western Suwŏn–Ch'ŏnan–Taejŏn axis, Task Force Smith, comprising 406 officers and other ranks from battalion headquarters company, half of the signals platoon, and below-strength B and C rifle companies was despatched from Japan. Lieutenant Colonel Charles B. Smith, commanding officer, 1st Battalion, 21st Regiment, US 24th Infantry Division, was tasked with executing a delaying action pending the arrival of the US 25th Infantry Division and the US 1st Cavalry Division.

Woefully underequipped, Smith's position near Suwŏn stood little chance against the Soviet-made North Korean T-34/85 tanks from the 107th Tank Regiment, KPA 105th Armoured Division at the head of the North Korean column. In the ensuing rout, the American task force ceased to be a recognizable combat unit. American troops abandoned their arms and equipment, bomb-shelling into the countryside.

Early in July, the UN Security Council called for international assistance, and General Douglas MacArthur was appointed commander of United Nations Command (UNC) forces to deal with the North Korean invasion. Soon thereafter, the US Eighth Army under Lieutenant General Walton Walker established its headquarters in South Korea. Towards the end of the month, combined American and South Korean forces had been unable to prevent the KPA from entering the Naktong River valley.

General Walton H. Walker, commander US Eighth Army, Korea.

By 4 August, General Walker had established a defensive enclave in the south-eastern corner of the peninsula that would gain fame as the Pusan Perimeter. From Masan in the south, north to Taegu, then east to P'ohang

> Walker skilfully and uniquely had utilized his limited resources by employing mobile combat tactics in rushing reserves to where his defence line came under the greatest threat at any one point in time. In partnership with indispensable naval and air support, without which the US Eighth Army would most likely have been overrun, Walker held out long enough to see his now flagging endurance finally stall the North Korean offensive around 12 September. The tide began to turn in the United Nations Command's favour.[*]

Against overwhelming odds, General Walker held the line, in the process eroding the resolve and capabilities of the North Koreans to push home their offensive. For MacArthur, the time had arrived to launch a daring, high-risk attack by sea on the invaders' right flank. There would be a simultaneous breakout from the Pusan Perimeter, entrapping the KPA.

On 15 September 1950, regiments of the US 1st Marine Division spearheaded the US X Corps amphibious landing at the west coast port of Inch'ŏn. With the beachhead secured, the US 7th Infantry Division commenced disembarking the following day. Without pausing, the Marines marched on Seoul while, to the south, General Walker initiated the planned breakout by sending the US 2nd Infantry Division out the perimeter to push the KPA back across the Naktong River.

After bitter street fighting in parts of Seoul, in the afternoon of 27 September elements of the US 5th Marines

> arrived at an empty Government House where, at 3.08 p.m., the American flag was raised in front of the imposing former Japanese General Government Building. By the end of the day—27 September—any semblance of North Korean resistance had ceased to exist, twelve days after MacArthur's Inch'ŏn gamble.[†]

Not satisfied with pushing the North Korean invaders back north of the 38th Parallel, the public acclaim that his military successes had attracted back home fuelled MacArthur's ardent desire to pursue the shattered KPA forces north of the 38th. His ultimate objective was to herd the enemy against the Yalu River border between Korea and Chinese Manchuria to totally neutralize any future North Korean threat.

However, in sub-zero winter temperatures that froze everything from vehicle engines to emergency medicines, MacArthur set his field commanders on a race for the Yalu. Whilst

---

[*] Gerry van Tonder, *North Korean Onslaught: UN Stand at the Pusan Perimeter, August–September 1950* (Pen and Sword Military, Barnsley, 2018).

[†] Gerry van Tonder, *Korean War, Inchonn Landing: MacArthur's Masterstroke, September 1950* (Pen and Sword Military, Barnsley, 2019).

acknowledging a limited Communist Chinese presence within KPA ranks, intelligence did not—or would not—raise the alarm to a substantial Chinese military threat on North Korean soil.

General Walker's US Eighth Army was to strike north overland along the Kaesŏng–Sariwŏn axis to take P'yŏngyang. The US X Corps, under Lieutenant General Edward M. Almond would effect an amphibious landing at the east coast port city of Wŏnsan, thereby establishing a line of defence across the Korean peninsula along a Chŏng-ju–Kunmŏ-ri–Yŏngwŏn–Hamhŭng–Hŭngnam axis. By 20 October, the ROKA 1st Infantry Division, and the US 1st Cavalry and 2nd Infantry divisions had secured the North Korean capital, P'yŏngyang.

At this time, General MacArthur issued fresh orders to all his ground commanders, rescinding previous related orders and lifting all restrictions on UN forces' deployments south of the Yalu River border. On 24 October, a signal from the JCS in Washington challenged MacArthur's radical deviation from the directive of 27 September. MacArthur had no problem justifying his decision, contending that military necessity, based on the inability of the South Koreans to sustain the offensive on their own, forced his change in the manner in which he had to prosecute the war. He also deemed it fit to remind his military supremos that the whole issue had been dealt with when he met with President Truman on Wake Island.[*]

In the fifth in a series of six books on the Korean War, the author looks at the costly and disastrous consequences of this misjudgement and impulsiveness:

Washington's miscalculations of China's intentions became rudely and painfully evident on 26 November when General Lin Piao's 'volunteers', in North Korea since mid-October, fell on the US I and IX corps, while simultaneously jumping off from Tŏkch'ŏn to plough through the Republic of Korea Army (ROKA) II Corps. The following two months witnessed the longest retreat in the history of the American military.[†]

The sheer magnitude of MacArthur's dramatic reversal of fortunes, characterized by high casualty numbers and mass evacuations, stunned the United States. In Washington, while the apportionment of blame for the Korean disaster dominated the offices of power, the US Strategic Air Command was placed on alert for an immediate deployment of medium bombers to the Far East. Should they go, it would be with atomic capabilities.

---

[*] Gerry van Tonder, *Korean War: Allied Surge: Pyongyang Falls, UN Sweep to the Yalu, October 1950* (Pen and Sword Military, Barnsley, 2019).

[†] Gerry van Tonder, *Korean War: Chinese Invasion: People's Liberation Army Crosses the Yalu October 1950—March 1951* (Pen and Sword Military, Barnsley, 2019).

General Douglas MacArthur.
(Photo NARA)

The conflict on the Korean peninsula would now centre on the 38th Parallel, where reduced combat capabilities on both sides gave rise to months of stalemate, in a perpetual cycle of fluctuating offence, defence and counter-offence.

As early as July 1951, all warring parties would meet to discuss the implementation of a ceasefire. However, it would be two years before terms for an armistice were agreed to, a period that would witness some of the fiercest fighting, heaviest loss of life and massive destruction of property. Imjin River, Gloster Hill, Heartbreak Ridge, Old Baldy, Hook and Pork Chop were names that would become synonymous with the quagmire of strategically indecisive battles along the 38th Parallel for more than two years.

1. RED SPRING OFFENSIVE

'The commanders and fighters of the entire Chinese People's Liberation Army absolutely must not relax in the least their will to fight; any thinking that relaxes the will to fight and belittles the enemy is wrong.'

Mao Zedong, 5 March 1949, *Selected Works*, Vol. IV

Early in January 1951, Lieutenant General Matthew B. Ridgway, the new commander of the US Eighth Army upon General Walker's death in a vehicle accident on 23 December 1950, developed a deliberate and aggressive offensive technique to restore military advantages along the frontline. In a predictable strategy employing maximum firepower, dubbed 'Meat Grinder', the attainment of specific objectives did not feature.

Ridgway started with Operation Killer, which drew the US I, IX and X corps together in a solid, lumbering phalanx during which a KPA salient into the UN lines was eradicated and Line Arizona restored and strengthened.

The successes of the new strategy could not yet be measured in absolute terms, but the robust shoulder-to-shoulder advance with massive artillery and close air support, destroying anything blocking its way, combined with the employment of maximum firepower from armour, mortars and machine guns, made for impregnable and seemingly unstoppable phase-line advances.

Buoyed by the strategic efficacy of the employment of this raw and brutal brand of warfare employed in Killer, Ridgway launched operations Ripper (6–31 March), Courageous (21–31 March), Rugged (3–6 April) and Dauntless (11–22 April) in quick succession.

Stretching across the entire front, almost all UN forces were employed and directed on successive predetermined phase lines as Ripper commenced on 7 March. Preceded by a pre-dawn 5,000-shell bombardment from 148 artillery pieces and 900 main-gun rounds from divisional armour, the US 25th Infantry Division, under Major General J. Sladen Bradley, crossed the Han River to gain Line Albany less than a week later.

On the right, the US 24th Infantry (Major General John H. Church), US 1st Cavalry (Major General Charles D. Palmer), ROKA 6th (Brigadier General Kim Jong-oh) and US 1st Marine (Major General Oliver P. Smith) divisions, and the 27th British Commonwealth Brigade (Brigadier Basil D. Coad), reached Line Albany at last light on 12 March. Next on the right were disposed the US 2nd Infantry (Major General Clark L. Ruffner), the US 7th Infantry (Major General Claude B. Ferenbaugh) and ROKA 5th (Major General Lee Ung Joon) divisions. To their right and to the coast, came the ROKA 7th (General Yu Jae Hung) and 9th Major General Kim Jong-oh) divisions and, finally, the ROKA Capital Division (General Lee Chong Chan).

Lieutenant General William M. Hoge, commanding US IX Corps, holds the lanyard for the 75,oooth shell to be fired by the corps since the start of the conflict in Korea, 25 June 1950. (Photo US Signals Corps).

U.N. LOSSES IN KOREA

The U.N. armies in Korea have lost more than 220,000 men killed, wounded and missing since the start of the war it was announced at 8th Army H.Q. to-day. Communist armies are claimed to have lost between 600,000 and 700,000 men.

Of the U.N. armies, South Korea has lost three men for every casualty suffered by all other U.N. armies. Altogether, South Korea has lost 169,000 in killed, wounded and missing. Apart from U.S. and South Korean casualties other U.N. contingents lost 2,800.

General MacArthur said in his communiqué to-day that the Red delaying action had been fought to screen the building up of nine to twelve fresh Chinese divisions immediately behind the present battle area.

Aberdeen Evening Express, 5 March 1951

By the end of 15 March, the US 25th had outflanked Seoul and the US 24th had attained the Ch'ŏngp'yŏng Reservoir. The US 1st Cavalry had reached the Hongch'ŏn River, while the ROKA 6th commanded high ground overlooking the river. Having met with stiff opposition, the US 1st Marines could only take the town of Hongch'ŏn and attain the river bank later in the day. Elements of the ROKA 1st Division entered Seoul on 14 March, to discover that the occupying enemy forces had withdrawn to a position 5 miles north of the city. The following day, the ROKA 1st and US 3rd divisions secured Seoul and immediately set about establishing defensible terrain to the north of the city.

By last light on 19 March, most of the US IX Corps had attained Line Buster-Buffalo, from where they advanced to Line Cairo and the unopposed capture of Ch'unch'ŏn two days later. By this time, in the east the US X and ROKA III corps had made Line Idaho to slot in on the US IX Corps' right flank. From here, the three UN corps deployed probing combat patrols well above the 38th Parallel between Ch'unch'ŏn and Hwach'ŏn Reservoir.

Operation Courageous was launched on 22 March to supplement Ripper. It was the intention that the US I Corps, to bring it in line with the US Eighth Army, would employ maximum strength and firepower to trap and annihilate 60,000 North Korean

Bunker clearing. (Photo USMC)

troops south of Imjin River. However, whilst territorial objectives were achieved, the KPA withdrew ahead of the US 187th Airborne Regimental Combat Team at Munsn-ni and Ŭijŏngbu where the North Koreans had opposed the ROKA 1st and US 3rd divisions respectively, thereby avoiding destruction.

Thus, by 1 April 1950, the US Eighth Army's twelve combat divisions were positioned along the 38th Parallel, leaving South Korea largely clear of enemy troops. Electing not to retain a static position, General Ridgway was granted authorization by General MacArthur to advance north of the 38th on the infamous Iron Triangle where twenty-seven CPVA and eighteen KPA divisions were concentrating in what military intelligence regarded as preparations for a spring offensive.

The Iron Triangle was the name given by the Western press to a key military concentration area and communications hub for the North Korean and Chinese forces. Located in the central sector 20 to 30 miles north of the 38th Parallel, the 'triangle' was delineated by P'yŏnggang (not to be confused with the capital P'yŏngyang) to the north, Ch'ŏrwŏn the west and Kimhwa in the east. The area was the scene of some of the bloodiest engagements of the Korean War between the CPVA and the US Eighth Army.

On 5 April, General Ridgway launched Operation Rugged across the peninsula: the US I Corps in the west, the US IX Corps in the centre, and the US X and ROKA I and III corps on the eastern flank of the UN defence line advanced on the newly created phase line, Kansas. With the line attained and his forces dug in, Ridgway introduced Line Utah, essentially a northward bulge of Kansas in the west. This placed UN troops just south of Ch'ŏrwŏn, the south-western anchor of the Iron Triangle.

Operation Dauntless followed, a two-phase operation designed to establish a 25-mile bulge in the direction of the Iron Triangle. As dawn broke on 11 April, US I Corps, commanded by Lieutenant General Frank W. Milburn and comprising the US 3rd, 24th and 25th and the ROKA 1st divisions, jumped off from the Imjin River line. Hampered by enemy sniper fire at the steep banks of the Hanta'an River crossing, some units were delayed until the following day, while others were able to advance into the Iron Triangle.

The second phase of Dauntless was initiated on 21 April when, on Ridgway's left flank centred on Seoul, the US I Corps advanced on Line Wyoming from their positions on Line Utah. In support, to the right US IX Corps moved from Line Kansas in the direction of Line Quantico, just north of Hwach'ŏn Reservoir. Here, the CPVA screened their strength and activities by starting widespread brush fires. A Chinese officer captured during an engagement revealed that the CPVA spring offensive was imminent.

Having taken a severe beating at Wŏnju and failing to dislodge UN forces at the key Chip'yŏng-ni junction, the CPVA broke off its fourth offensive around 18 February, and withdrew to regroup. Units that had participated in the opening phases of the Chinese invasion, such as the CPVA XXXVIII, XXXIX, XL and XLII corps, had been withdrawn but remained south of the Yalu River. The CPVA L and LXVI corps returned to China to be reconstituted.

US 3rd Infantry Division troops before setting off on an Imjin River patrol, 17 April 1951. (Photo US Signals Corps)

The CPVA Third, Ninth and Nineteenth armies now crossed into North Korea from Manchuria. The Third and Nineteenth were freshly equipped with Soviet weaponry, allowing for each of the two corps to include an artillery regiment and an anti-aircraft gun battalion, while each regiment incorporated a recoilless gun company, an anti-aircraft gun company and a 120-mm mortar company.

By 6 April 1951, CPVA commander Marshal Peng Dehuai had officially mapped out his order of battle and deployments for the launch of the spring offensive on 22 April. Totalling an estimated 340,000 troops (other estimates put the figure at 250,000), Peng would commit nine CPVA corps in the attack, of which six corps were to strike directly at the US Eighth Army's I Corps above Seoul. The CPVA LXIII Corps was tasked with attacking the ROKA 1st Division and the British 29th (Independent) Brigade (29th British) defending the US I Corps' left flank along the Imjin River. To the immediate east, the CPVA would focus their attentions on the relatively weak ROKA 6th Division on the US IX Corps' left flank in the Kap'yŏng sector. The objectives would be to envelop the US I and IX corps, cut the trans-peninsular Seoul-to-Kansŏng highway and to retake the South Korean capital. At 10 p.m. on 22 April, the US Eighth Army came under a major attack along a 40-mile UN front defending Seoul to the north.

CPVA commander Peng Dehuai with Chen Geng (left) and Deng Hua (right).

While Peng sat around a strategic map with his commanders in early April, in Washington the embarrassing defeats at the hands of Mao's armed peasant hordes brought the simmering question over General MacArthur's competence to a head. Since the strained meeting at Wake Island on 15 October 1950, the divergent views of President Truman and the commander of the UN forces in Korea, had grown to untenable proportions. MacArthur's belief in his own invincibility and therefore that of his troops was intertwined with his intransigent behaviour and disdain for those in authority above him.

The remarkable successes at Inch'ŏn and Pusan contributed considerably to MacArthur's egotistical persona. The question of the employment of nuclear weapons against North Korea—and later China—remained an important factor in the acrimonious Truman/MacArthur relationship. As far back as the Federalist essays of the late 1700s, there had been a powerful constitutional argument in the United States for the distribution of power among the executive, the legislature and the judiciary, with an emphasis on civilian control to preserve liberty and democracy. Any national decisions to declare war, conduct an invasion or end a conflict would all have a profound impact on the nation's civilians. The Second World War French prime minister, Georges Clemenceau, is often cited as having said, 'War is too serious a matter to entrust to military men,' and 'War is too important to be left to the generals.'

On 9 July 1950, the day after MacArthur's appointment as commander of UN forces in Korea, the US Joint Chiefs of Staff (JCS) decided to sound out MacArthur as to the

US President Harry S. Truman at Wake Island, about to present a Distinguished Service Medal to General Douglas MacArthur, October 1950. (Photo Truman Library)

possible use of nuclear weapons. The general was in favour of such use, but for tactical purposes to destroy enemy infrastructure such as bridges and tunnels. His views were deemed impractical.

At a press conference on 30 November 1950, President Truman was asked if his administration was contemplating using the atomic bomb in Korea. Truman's response that the military would make that decision was rapidly clarified by a White House statement that 'only the President can authorize the use of the atom bomb, and no such authorization has been given'.*

On 6 April, Truman met with the chairman of the United States Atomic Energy Commission, Gordon Dean, to arrange for the transfer of nine Mark 4 nuclear bombs to military control. With a diameter of 60 inches, the Mark 4 was an implosion-type device based on the design of the Mark 3 'Fat Man' bomb that had destroyed the Japanese city of Nagasaki on 9 August 1945. Reflecting on events in Korea immediately prior to April 1951,

---

* 'The President's News Conference', 30 November 1950, Harry S. Truman Library and Museum.

Atomic cloud over Nagasaki from Koyagi-jima, by Hiromichi Matsuda, 9 August 1945. (Photo Nagasaki Atomic Bomb Museum)

MacArthur made it clear in an interview in January 1954 that he was a proponent of the multiple employment of atomic bombs in a tactical capacity:

> Of all the campaigns of my life, 20 major ones to be exact, the one I felt most sure of was the one I was deprived of waging. I could have won the war in Korea in a maximum of 10 days. I would have dropped between 30 and 50 atomic bombs on his [the enemy's] air bases and other depots strung across the neck of Manchuria.
>
> It was my plan as our amphibious forces moved south to spread behind us—from the Sea of Japan to the Yellow Sea—a belt of radioactive cobalt. It could have been spread from wagons, carts, trucks and planes. For at least 60 years there could have been no land invasion of Korea from the north. The enemy could not have marched across that radiated belt.*

Both Dean and the JCS, however, had serious reservations about allowing MacArthur anywhere near the nuclear button, so consequently placed the nuclear strike force under the Strategic Air Command (SAC). Nuclear-capable Boeing B-29 bombers of the

---

* 'Texts of Accounts by Lucas and Considine on Interviews with MacArthur in 1954', *New York Times*, 9 April 1964.

US 9th Bombardment Wing would transfer atomic bombs without their fissile cores to Guam until the end of the war.

On 24 March 1951, General MacArthur made a public announcement that was, for his president, the last straw. Pre-empting an imminent statement by President Truman on the war, MacArthur put it to China that its military weakness was the cause of its inability to conquer Korea. In what amounted to an unashamed ultimatum, before offering to meet Chinese commanders in the field to discuss an end to hostilities, MacArthur's stated:

[China] must by now be painfully aware that a decision of the United Nations to depart from its tolerant effort to contain the war to the area of Korea, through an expansion of our military operations to its coastal areas and interior bases, would doom Red China to the risk of imminent military collapse.[*]

News of MacArthur's unauthorized statement was received with apoplexy in the Oval Office. He had deliberately usurped the powers of the civilian head of state enshrined in Article II of the Constitution, anathema to the very foundation of citizen democracy and the responsibility for the defence of both the nation and liberty. Beijing, puzzled that Washington's foreign policy should suddenly spring from such an unlikely source, viewed MacArthur's naïve statement as a challenge to strengthen its own resolve. Radio Peking broadcast:

Warmonger MacArthur made a fanatical but shameless statement with the intention of engineering the Anglo-American aggressors to extend the war of aggression into China . . . MacArthur's shameless tricks . . . will meet with failure. The people of China must raise their sense of vigilance by doubling their effort for the sacred struggle.[†]

Until 5 April, it was generally felt that the importance of MacArthur's 24 March faux pas had been largely overlooked in favour of more urgent developments on the Korean peninsula. However, on 5 April, Republican House Minority Leader Joseph W. Martin, an ardent foe of Democratic Party administrations, stood up in the House of Representatives and divulged the contents of a letter of 21 March from MacArthur, which read in part:

It seems strangely difficult for some to realize that here in Asia is where the Communist conspirators have elected to make their play for global conquest, and that we have joined the issue thus raised on the battlefield; that here we fight Europe's war with arms while the diplomats there still fight it with words; that if we lose this war to Communism in Asia the fall of Europe is inevitable; win it and Europe most probably would avoid war and yet preserve freedom. As you pointed out, we must win. There is no substitute for victory.[‡]

---

[*] James McGovern, *To the Yalu, From the Chinese Invasion of Korea to MacArthur's Dismissal.* (William Morrow, New York, 1972).

[†] Ibid.

[‡] Ibid.

Truman needed no further prompting to immediately work towards a decision on MacArthur's future in the Korean conflict. The very next morning—Friday 6 April— after Martin's revelation, Secretary of State Dean Acheson, Chairman of the JCS General Omar N. Bradley, Secretary of Defense George C. Marshall, and national security advisor W. Averell Harriman were called to the Oval Office to discuss MacArthur's future.

Understandably, there was a consensus, but one with individual caveats. Marshall cautioned against a quick decision, requesting time to consider the issue further. Bradley accepted that there was a case for insubordination that warranted dismissal, but declared that he could not offer any recommendations until he had conferred with his JCS colleagues. Acheson opined that MacArthur's rebellious behaviour was adequate reason to relieve the general from all of his many commands and his removal from the Far East, but that such a move would result in major upheaval in Washington. Only Harriman came out with a very clear opinion: MacArthur should have been dismissed two years ago.

Reconvening after a cabinet meeting at which the MacArthur conundrum was not raised, Truman asked Marshall to study all Pentagon files holding communications with MacArthur over the previous two years. Bradley was tasked with meeting with the rest

President Truman with his some of his top advisers, upon his return to Washington from Wake Island. From left: Averell Harriman, George C. Marshall, Truman, Dean Acheson, Secretary of the Treasury John Snyder, Secretary of the Army Frank Pace, Jnr., General Omar Bradley. (Photo NARA)

Ground crew members, such as these pictured during winter at K-10 (Chinhae) airfield, performed magnificently in primitive and tough conditions. (SAAF Museum)

of the JCS and to bring with him the body's recommendations at the next meeting scheduled for Monday morning, 9 April.

At that meeting, the recommendation to relieve MacArthur's of all his commands was unanimous. Truman selected Secretary of the Army Frank Pace to personally deliver the orders to MacArthur in Tokyo. However, before Pace could fly to Tokyo, on 11 April a special radio bulletin from Washington announced that Truman had removed MacArthur from his Far East and Korean commands and from occupied Japan. It was indeed unfortunate that General of the Army Douglas MacArthur, Supreme Commander Allied Powers Japan, Commander-in-Chief United Nations Command, Korea, and Commander-in-Chief Far East, should learn of the termination of a 52-year military career from a radio broadcast.

MacArthur later wrote that 'No office boy, no charwoman, no servant of any sort would have been dismissed with such callous disregard for the ordinary decencies . . . my abrupt relief when victory was in my grasp'.* At a special news conference at 1 a.m. on 11 April, called to minimize the fallout from MacArthur's leaked dismissal, Truman explained that the general 'is unable to give his wholehearted support to the policies of the United States Government and of the United nations in matters pertaining to his duties'.†

In Korea, General Ridgway received orders that he would assume all of MacArthur's commands, relinquishing his position as commander of the US Eighth Army to General James A. Van Fleet. A veteran of the Normandy invasion, and with a reputation as a forceful, courageous and competent commander, Van Fleet ended the Second World War in Europe as commander of the US III Corps with the rank of major general.

---

* Ibid.
† Ibid.

2. TRAPPED ON THE IMJIN

'The men of The Gloucestershire Regiment dying like the Spartans at Thermopylae, were true to a glorious tradition—the tradition of the British Regiments of the Line, the first Infantry in the world.'

Illustrated London News, 19 May 1951

Rising in the Taebaek Mountains west of the North Korean east coast port of Wŏnsan, the 159-mile-long Imjin River flows in a southerly direction, before turning south-west and disgorging into the Yellow Sea north-west of Seoul. Its proximity to the South Korean capital made it an important defensive line for UN forces during the Korean War. It was therefore also of equal strategic importance to the combined Chinese and North Korean forces, with the capture of Seoul as a prime objective in the latest fifth, or spring, offensive of 22–30 April 1951.

As at 22 April, General Van Fleet, newly appointed commander of the US Eighth Army, had his forces dug in on Line Kansas. From Munsan-ni near the mouth of the Imjin River, to just west of the Kap'yŏng River was the US I Corps sector. From west to east, the US I Corps line was held by the ROKA 1st Division, and the US 3rd, 24th and 25th infantry divisions.

On 30 March, the British 29th (Independent) Infantry Brigade was assigned to the US 3rd Infantry Division (US 3rd). With the unflattering nickname of 'Frozen Arsehole', the brigade was re-activated after the outbreak of the Korean War to augment the United Nations war effort, arriving in Korea in December 1950. Division commander Major General Robert H. Soule, in working out his troop dispositions, viewed his front along the Imjin River between Korangp'o-ri and Route 33—his main line of communication—to be particularly vulnerable to enemy attack.

He placed the US 65th Regiment, with the attached Philippine 10th Battalion Combat Team, on the right half of the line. The 2nd and 3rd battalions would face north and north-west along the Imjin, with the Filipinos straddling Route 33 on the right flank. The 1st Battalion would be held in regimental reserve along Route 33 just to the north of the Hant'an River. The 29th British were to hold the rest of the line.

Commanded by Brigadier Thomas Brodie, the 29th British comprised the 1st Battalion, Royal Northumberland Fusiliers (1/RNF), 1st Battalion, the Gloucestershire Regiment (1/Glosters), 1st Battalion, the Royal Ulster Rifles (1/RUR), 8th King's Royal Irish Hussars (8/RIH), C Squadron, 7th Royal Tank Regiment (7/RTR), the 45th Field Regiment, RA, 11 LAA Battery, RA, and 170 Mortar Battery, RA. It also included elements of non-British forces, such as the Belgian United Nations Command (BUNC), a combined Belgium/Luxembourg battalion under Lieutenant Colonel Albert Crahay. (see a map of the 29th British sector in the colour plate section)

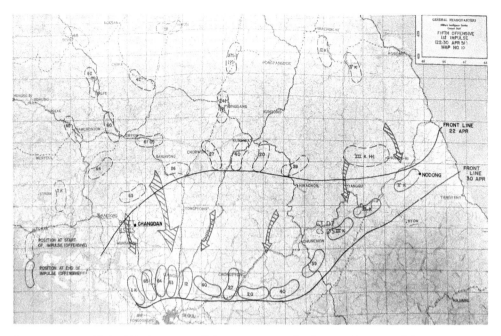

A contemporary United Nations map of the trans-peninsular front at the time of the CPVA spring offensive, 22–30 April 1951.

To the right, the 27th British Commonwealth Brigade (27th British) had been attached to the US IX Corps and disposed near Kap'yŏng on the Kansas Line. Originally activated in August 1950, two Hong Kong-based battalions, the 1st Battalion, the Argyll and Sutherland Highlanders (1/Argylls), and the 1st Battalion, the Middlesex Regiment (1/Middlesex), were the first British combat troops of the Korean War. A month later, the 3rd Battalion, the Royal Australian Regiment (3/RAR) joined the brigade.

Commanded by Brigadier Basil Coad since October 1950, the 27th British had gained considerable combat experience from the Pusan Perimeter breakout to the taking of P'yŏngyang. Early in 1951, the brigade's strength was bolstered by the attachment of the 16 Field Regiment, Royal New Zealand Artillery (16/RNZA) and the 2nd Battalion, Princess Patricia's Canadian Light Infantry (2/PPCLI). On 25 April, the 27th British was disbanded and replaced by the fully constituted 28th British Commonwealth Infantry Brigade (28th British), part of the 1st Commonwealth Division.

At 10 p.m. on 22 April, under a full moon the sounds of bugles and horns and the firing of flares heralded the start of the main CPVA offensive. Along the US 3rd and US 25th infantry divisions' line on the Imjin River, 40,000 screaming troops from the CPVA Nineteenth and Third armies attacked. The 187th, 188th and 189th divisions of the CPVA LXIII Corps and the 198th Division from the CPVA LX Corps had been ordered to breach the UN line and destroy the 29th British.

Earlier that night, 1/RNF and BUNC listening posts had detected enemy activity on the north bank of the Imjin, but brigade HQ had not anticipated anything serious during the night. Brigadier Brodie had issued two orders: place a company and a mobile battle patrol of the 1/RUR on standby, and the 1/RNF to prepare a company-sized patrol to cross the Imjin in the morning.

Lieutenant-Colonel James Power Carne, commanding officer of the 1/Glosters, was more astute. That afternoon, CPVA parties had been observed approaching Gloster Crossing through the Imjin, causing Carne to place his battalion on 50 per cent standby for immediate combat. The routine nightly listening post would still be deployed, but an ambush would also be set up in anticipation of an enemy crossing. A sixteen-man patrol, drawn from C Company and led by Lieutenant Guy Temple, was given the task, with the specific brief of capturing a Chinese soldier for interrogation purposes.

Transported by Oxford carrier to riverbank entrenchments to the right of Gloster Crossing, the unit was heavily armed with three Bren machine guns and 4,000 rounds of .303 ammunition, a large stock of mortar bombs and six hand grenades per soldier. At around 11.30 p.m., Temple fired a flare in response to noise in the river below, illuminating a small group of Chinese troops wading through the river. The Glosters laid down a

Korean War Victoria Cross recipient Lieutenant-Colonel James Power Carne, commanding officer of the 1st Battalion, the Gloucestershire Regiment.

curtain of fire, the enemy bomb-shelled, and stillness returned. But moments later, a second flare revealed large numbers of the enemy making the crossing.

Temple immediately radioed battalion HQ for artillery support. After a brief spell of registration, 25-pounders from a battery of the British 45th Field Regiment started to zero in on the crossing. However, the impact on what had become an estimated brigade-strength crossing was minimal, so Temple called for 'Mike Target' maximum artillery support. At this, all twenty-four artillery pieces of the 45th Field Regiment were brought to bear on Gloster Crossing. Despite a massive expenditure of ammunition and mortars by Temple's men, the Chinese started to clamber up the south bank. In the hopeless situation, Temple received permission to withdraw to the main battalion line.

On the brigade's right flank, Colonel Crahay's Belgian battalion suddenly also came under threat from overwhelming numbers of advancing Chinese troops. Crahay called for defensive artillery support from the 45th Field Regiment, to supplement the fire from 170 Mortar Battery attached to his battalion. Around midnight, the CPVA penetrated the Belgian's C Company position, occupying a bunker.

In anticipation of a Belgian withdrawal under the codeword 'Foxhound', Brodie committed his reserve battalion, the 1/RUR, to ensure the Belgians' line of retreat was kept clear. Sitting 5 miles south of Ulster Crossing through the Imjin River and watching an open-air movie, the Irish were oblivious to the fact that the CPVA had already taken the crossing. Only the sudden sounds and accompanying pyrotechnics of fierce

CPVA troops, each armed with a Soviet-made PPSh-41 sub-machine gun, undergo Maoist indoctrination before going into battle.

fighting immediately to the north made acting commander Major Gerald Rickord realize that the line was under threat. He would despatch a battle patrol in Oxford carriers north to secure the bridges over the Imjin. Once the troop carriers returned, he would fight his way forward to the BUNC position.

At 2 a.m., battle patrol commander Lieutenant Hedley Craig stopped the eight carriers on the south bank and debussed his fifty-strong unit. Strangely, they were met with silence and no sign of any enemy activity. Climbing back onto the Oxfords, Craig took the patrol over the vehicle bridge, where he unwittingly drove straight into a CPVA ambush on the north bank. Trapped in a massive barrage of enemy fire, the patrol stood little chance. Escape was the only option. A covering party was hastily knocked together, but only one Oxford and six wounded men initially made it back to the south bank.

In the early hours of 23 April, at his brigade command post Brigadier Brodie faced the fact that his whole brigade front was under heavy CPVA attack. Not only were the three Belgian companies out on a limb north of the Imjin, but at their position on Hill 196 each company had been cut off from the other and from battalion command post. Crahay's position was desperate, not being able to control or direct the situation through not knowing the status of each of his companies or that of the bridge across the Imjin, his only route of retreat.

Across the Imjin, 3 miles to the south-west, X Company, 1/RNF, commanded by Major Reginald Pratt, came under attack from several quarters. While 6 Platoon had an initial brief engagement with the CPVA, the brunt of the Chinese attack was on 4 Platoon, which lost more than half of its strength in less than three hours. The platoon's fighting timbre evaporated and the survivors fled, exposing 5 Platoon's flank and placing the whole of X Company's defensive position in great peril. At 2.15 a.m., 1/RNF commanding officer, Lieutenant-Colonel Kingsley Foster, gave Pratt permission to withdraw as and when it became necessary—his other two companies were under the same threat.

A mile to the east of X Company, on Hill 217 W Company was under attack from all sides, but were able to hold their position. To the right, 11 Platoon, Z Company, came under surprise attack on Hill 257, forcing them to abandon the position shortly before 5 a.m. At this time battalion HQ came under enemy fire, prompting Colonel Foster to withdraw south to the relative safety of a defended position provided by Centurion Mk. III tanks of C Squadron, 7/RTR.

With the CPVA seizure of Hill 257, 70 Field Battery, 45th Field Regiment, came under direct threat. While continuing to provide support to the 1/Glosters, battery commander Lieutenant George Truell levelled one of his guns to fire over open sights at Chinese attackers only 150 yards off. Twenty minutes of fire was sufficient to momentarily deter his assailants.

Three miles off on the 1/RNF's left flank, the 1/Glosters were coming under increasing pressure as the CPVA 187th Regiment forced Carne's company dispositions.

British Centurion Mk. 3 main battle tanks and troops of the Gloucestershire Regiment advancing on Hill 327, March 1951. (Photo MoD)

While brigade artillery stalled the CPVA at Gloster Crossing, the battalion was unaware that the enemy was pouring across at a hitherto unknown ford a short distance upstream.

Around midnight, A Company on Castle Hill (Hill 148)—the farthest north of the 1/Glosters—bore the brunt of the Chinese assault, followed by D Company on Hill 182 a mile off on their right. After a few hours, on the battalion right flank B Company also came under attack as the CPVA ploughed their way south. Despite the Glosters throwing everything they had at the Chinese and inflicting enormous casualties on the enemy, the waves of PPSh-firing, screaming and grenade-lobbing CPVA were endless.

As the long night progressed, Brigadier Brodie was increasingly cognizant of the gravity of the situation facing his command. The collapse of the 1/RNF sector would mean the certain result of the CPVA cutting Route 11 to the south, and from there Route 33, the main supply route. Brodie accepted that the 1/Glosters position at Solma-ri covered the less important Route 5Y, but his greater concern was that the loss of this sector would expose the ROKA 1st Division's right flank, while exerting greater pressure on the 1/RNF to the east.

As a consequence, and while the Belgians clung on north of the Imjin, Brodie believed that it was his responsibility to hold the brigade sector to protect the UN forces on either flank. No orders for withdrawal had been received at brigade HQ, nor would Brodie push for permission to fall back.

USAF Douglas B-26B Invaders of the 452nd Bombardment Wing returning from a mission over North Korea, May 1951. (Photo USAF)

The commander's initial thinking was to split his reserves, the 1/RUR, to bolster the 1/Glosters and 1/RNF positions: A and D companies to support the 1/RNF and to prepare to retake the Imjin bridges, and B and C companies to be on immediate standby for a counterattack in support of 1/Glosters. Daylight would bring a change in circumstances, with air support, the employment of the 7/RTR Centurions and, hopefully, the CPVA would typically break off contact with the dawn of a new day. As the sun rose on 23 April, in a conversation with battalion chaplain Padre Sam Davies, 1/Glosters Regimental Sergeant-Major Jack Hobbs commented, 'They'll give up at dawn. Mark my words, sir; they'll go back across the river.'*

During that first night, FEAF conducted successful radar-controlled night-bombing sorties against the advancing Chinese forces. Having arrived in Korea in October 1950, the US 502nd Tactical Air Control Group (US 502/TACG) had one of its squadrons operating a Tactical Air Control Centre (TACC), while the other three established Tactical Air Direction Centres (TADCs) at Kimp'o, Taegu and Taejon. The following month, as the US Eighth Army crossed into North Korea, the US 502/TACG had established a direction centre at Sinanju, from where it directed Douglas B-26 Invader light bomber and ground attack aircraft strikes in support of advancing ground troops.

---

* S.P. MacKenzie, *The Imjin and Kapyong Battle, Korea, 1951* (Indiana University Press, Bloomington, 2013).

In January 1951, the group tried out a new type of control system, the Tactical Air Direction Post (TADP), dubbed 'Tadpoles'. Each of the US I, IX and X corps received one such forward control unit in close support. Truck-mounted AN/MPQ-2 radar systems enabled the operator to manually plot an enemy target on the 'Blind Bombing Plotting Sheet', which would then be applied to the manual E6B computer and bombing tables to calculate a release point for hitting the target. Using the MPQ to lock onto the bomber's flight path, the radar operator was then able to control the bomb run from the ground up to the release point. The system proved highly successful during night operations and in bad weather.

CPVA TACTICS

Because the enemy force, though small, is strong (in equipment and the training of officers and men) while our own force, though big, is weak (only in equipment and the training of officers and men but not in morale), we should, in campaign and battle operations, not only employ a big force to attack from an exterior line a small force on the interior line, but also adopt the aim of quick decision. To achieve quick decision we should generally attack, not an enemy force holding a position, but one on the move. We should have concentrated, beforehand under cover, a big force along the route through which the enemy is sure to pass, suddenly descend on him while he is moving, encircle and attack him before he knows what is happening, and conclude the fighting with all speed. If the battle is well fought, we may annihilate the entire enemy force or the greater part or a part of it. Even if the battle is not well fought, we may still inflict heavy casualties.

We say that it is easy to attack an enemy on the move precisely because he is then not on the alert, that is, he is inadvertent. These two things—creating illusions for the enemy and springing surprise attacks on him—are used to make the enemy face the uncertainties of war while securing for ourselves the greatest possible certainty of gaining superiority, initiative, and victory.

Mao Zedong, *On the Protracted War*, republished in China in 1951.

At first light, FEAF flew the first of 1,100 close-support sorties for 23 April, of which 340 were in support of the US Eighth Army. Smoke and haze from fires deliberately started by the CPVA failed to mask their movements from devastating American air power. In one incident early that afternoon, two Lockheed F-80 Shooting Stars of the 35th Fighter-Bomber Squadron, US 8th Operations Group, flying in close support over the Imjin River, observed around 200 CPVA troops trying to conceal themselves on the ground.

A US Air Force Lockheed F-80C Shooting Star, armed with napalm bombs, takes off from a Korean airfield, 1951. (Photo NARA)

The two American jets dropped four 260-lb bombs, fired eight 'Holy Moses' HVAR rockets and discharged 3,600 .50-calibre rounds, inflicting an estimated 175 enemy casualties.

To the US I Corps' right, General Hoge needed to consolidate his US IX Corps dispositions. During the night, troops of the ROKA 6th Division had scattered into neighbouring sectors, forcing commander General Chang to waste valuable time reassembling his men before following Hoge's orders to move three miles to the north onto Line Kansas. Turning to the US 1st Marine Division, Hoge wanted General Smooth to withdraw against the Pukhan River so as to create a juncture with the South Koreans via a line near the Hwach'on Reservoir. The imperative was to plug the gap between the two divisions.

Back in the US I Corps sector, by daylight the CPVA had penetrated 3 miles through the centre of the US 24th Division. The spearhead of the 59th Division, CPVA XX Corps, had forged a gap between the US 19th and 5th regiments, pushing behind a battalion of the US 19th and forcing the adjacent battalion of the US 5th to fall back almost a mile. Divisional commander Major General Blackshear M. Bryan was too late to deploy part of his reserve US 21st Regiment onto high ground to the north of Line Kansas as the CPVA had already seized control. Bryan's only available option was to pull his line regiments down the sides of the CPVA salient to make a stand.

33

South of Ch'ŏrwŏn, during the night the CPVA 2nd Motorized Artillery Division had executed a three-hour bombardment on US 25th Division positions, concentrating most of its shelling on the Turkish brigade along Route 33. Elements of the 179th Division, CPVA LX Corps, then hit the Turks, their attack spilling over into the US 24th in the division centre. The Turks collapsed, allowing the CPVA to push the US 24th's left flank all of 2 miles behind the divisional line. Addressing the deteriorating situation that threatened to become a rout, US 25th commander Major General J. Sladen Bradley pulled the US 24th and 27th regiments 2 miles south, while drawing the US 35th Regiment out of reserve to assume control of the Turkish sector. As the remnants of the Turkish brigade regrouped south of Hant'an, the Chinese broke off their pursuit and Bradley's sector became quiet.

Not certain of how exactly the Belgian brigade was going to extricate itself from the Imjin angle, General Soule went ahead to plan, pulling back his US 3rd Division's right flank forces. With the US 7th Regiment securing his eastern sector, covered to the west by the BUNC, the US 65th Regiment would jump off from Line Utah, pass through the US 7th, and assemble in division reserve near the junction of routes 33 and 11.

Encountering no interference from the direction of the beleaguered Belgians who were engaged in a bitter fight for survival, the 3rd Battalion, US 65th, together with the

A USMC M46 Patton medium tank with the Turkish Brigade. (Photo Master Sergeant J.W. Hayes)

3rd Reconnaissance Company and the 64th Tank Battalion (M46 Patton medium tanks), blocked Route 33 just above Hant'an, pending the withdrawal of the Belgians from Hill 194.

At around 2 p.m., the 1st Battalion, US 7th and a platoon of tanks moved up Route 11 to facilitate the Belgians' withdrawal. On reaching a point behind 1/RNF, in a gap with 1/Glosters, the battalion's three rifle companies commenced a sweep across a wide front on the slopes of Hill 257. At 6 p.m., battalion commander Lieutenant Colonel Fred C. Weyand concentrated his three companies to launch an attack on the hill.

As Weyand cleared the 1/RNF–1/RUR lines, the battalion came under heavy fire on both flanks and from the front. Two hours later, the battalion had made little progress, but the diversion was sufficient for the Belgians to move off the rear of Hill 194 and cross the Imjin River bridge under artillery and air cover. From here the motorized column cleared the Hant'an to move on to an assembly point at the junction of routes 11 and 33. The US 7th broke off their attack on Hill 257 and, returning to their position on Line Kansas, went into reserve.

The dangers are great. Make no mistake about it. Behind the North Koreans and Chinese Communists in the front lines stand additional millions of Chinese soldiers. And behind the Chinese stand the tanks, the planes, the submarines, the soldiers, and the scheming rulers of the Soviet Union.

Our aim is to avoid the spread of the conflict.

The course we have been following is the one best calculated to avoid an all-out war. It is the course consistent with our obligation to do all we can to maintain international peace and security. Our experience in Greece and Berlin shows that it is the most effective course of action we can follow.

First of all, it is clear that our efforts in Korea can blunt the will of the Chinese Communists to continue the struggle. The United Nations forces have put up a tremendous fight in Korea and have inflicted very heavy casualties on the enemy. Our forces are stronger now than they have been before. These are plain facts which may discourage the Chinese Communists from continuing their attack.

Second, the free world as a whole is growing in military strength every day. In the United States, in Western Europe, and throughout the world, free men are alert to the Soviet threat and are building their defenses. This may discourage the Communist rulers from continuing the war in Korea—and from undertaking new acts of aggression elsewhere.

If the Communist authorities realize that they cannot defeat us in Korea, if they realize it would be foolhardy to widen the hostilities beyond Korea, then they may recognize the folly of continuing their aggression. A peaceful settlement may then be possible. The door is always open.

President Harry S. Truman radio address to the
American people on Korea, 11 April 1951

A disabled British Centurion tank at Imjin River. (Photo Phillip Oliver Hobson)

During this time, the CPVA LXIV and LXIII corps had been building up their forces below the Imjin to the front and flanks of the 1/Glosters. Before daylight, A Company had been particularly hard hit in their position on Castle Hill (Hill 148). As dawn approached, the Chinese took the summit, but company commander Major Pat Angier was not ready to capitulate. He tasked one of his remaining officers, 24-year-old Lieutenant Philip Kenneth Edward Curtis (on attachment from the Duke of Cornwall's Light Infantry), to scrape together the remnants of 1 and 2 platoons to neutralize an enemy machine gun in an observation-post bunker just below the summit. With only 70 Field Battery in support—the USAF was committed elsewhere—Curtis led his party forward. However, running out of bazooka projectiles meant that open ground would have to be crossed to lob grenades into the enemy bunker. Curtis's posthumous Victoria Cross citation relates what happened next:

> Lieutenant CURTIS ordered some of his men to give him covering fire while he himself rushed the main position of resistance; in this charge Lieutenant CURTIS was severely wounded by a grenade. Several of his men crawled out and pulled him back under cover but, recovering himself, Lieutenant CURTIS insisted on making a second attempt. Breaking free from the men who wished to restrain him, he made another desperate charge, hurling grenades as he went, but was killed by a burst of fire when within a few yards of his objective.
>
> Although the immediate objective of this counter-attack was not achieved, it had yet a great effect on the subsequent course of the battle; for although the enemy had gained a footing on a position vital to the defence of the whole Company area, this success had resulted in such furious reaction that they made no further effort to exploit their success in this immediate area; had they done so, the eventual withdrawal of the Company might well have proved impossible.
>
> Lieutenant CURTIS's conduct was magnificent throughout this bitter battle.*

By this time, Colonel Carne had moved battalion HQ to the summit of Hill 235 held by C Company. It was here that battalion adjutant Captain Tony Farrar-Hockley answered a call on the radio from Major Angier calling for urgent reinforcements if he were to hold their position. Carne was left with a virtual no-win decision to make. His two forward companies, A and D, although weakened, prevented the CPVA from outflanking units of the ROKA 1st Division on his left and the 1/RNF his right. Added to this, brigade required him to hold Route 5Y from Chŏksŏng to Sŏlma-ri. In one of the most difficult decisions of his military life, Carne ordered Angier to hold his position at all costs. At brigade HQ, with the BUNC and 1/RNF in serious trouble, Brigadier Brodie was unable to strengthen the Glosters.

At 8 a.m. on 23 April, Carne ordered A and D companies to withdraw. The remaining fifty-seven members of A Company would leave first under cover from D Company on Hill 182. With artillery and mortar support, D Company followed, to assemble with A Company near Sŏlma-ri. The Chinese did not press home their attack on the retreating Glosters.

Redeploying B Company to Hill 314 from Hill 144, Carne sent A and D companies up to Hill 235, still held by C and Support companies. Situated some 2,000 yards from Hill 314, the new battalion stronghold soon became known as Gloster Hill.

The CPVA now skirted the 1/Glosters positions along high ground to cut off the battalion's line of retreat down Route 5Y. It would soon be learned that the Glosters F Echelon, 5 miles to the rear, had been overrun, effectively meaning that the Glosters were

---

* *The London Gazette* (Supplement), No. 40029, 27 November 1953.

An officer of the 1st Battalion, Gloucestershire Regiment, indicates to a military observer the area on Gloster Hill where the Glosters fought against CPVA forces in April 1951. This photo was taken five weeks after the battle.

surrounded. On the brigade's right, Brodie was also fighting a losing battle. Y Company, 1/RNF was under attack in an isolated bend of the Imjin River, the situation demanding battalion commander Lieutenant-Colonel Kingsley Foster's immediate attention. Contact was established with a troop of 8/RIH tanks to provide cover as Y Company made a fighting withdrawal. The outcome would be tragic.

As a result of a preventable misunderstanding, the commander of the tank troop believed the troops on top of an adjacent hill to be Chinese and those at the bottom to be friendly forces. Consequently, Y Company suffered serious blue-on-blue casualties from 20-lb shells and fire from BESA 7.92-mm machine guns.

That afternoon—23 April—after a failed counterattack by Z Company to regain Hill 257, Brigadier Brodie arrived at the 1/RNF HQ to personally order all four companies to withdraw to the south: Y and W companies to high ground on the right of Route 11 and X and Z companies farther down the valley.

General Milburn had by now ordered his US I Corps to retire to Line Kansas. By the end of the day, the US 65th Regiment to the right of the 29th British had, under close air support, withdrawn to the south of the Hant'an tributary of the Imjin. The Belgians were safe, and despite the fact that the CPVA 187th and 189th divisions were now ensconced on commanding ground south of the Imjin, the 1/RNF on high ground to the left and the 1/RUR on Hill 398 to the right essentially blocked CPVA direct access to Route 11. That afternoon the 10th Philippine Battalion Combat Team (10/BCT), a battery of self-propelled guns, and a company of M24 Chaffee light tanks and armoured cars had been transferred to the 29th British as a reserve force. However, with nightfall looming, Brodie was not prepared to risk sending the Filipinos up the narrow Route 5Y to support the isolated Glosters.

During the night of 23/24 April, the CPVA fell on the 29th British line with renewed vigour. To the east of Route 11, Y Company, 1/RNF, came under heavy attack. With both the company commander and his second-in-command wounded, the company withdrew from its hill position. While W Company was unsuccessful in retaking Y Company's old position, the unit dug in for the night on the 1/RNF flank, protecting the battalion from attack in the darkness.

On the brigade's left, however, the 1/Glosters position at Solma-ri came under fresh CPVA 187th Division attack, as the CPVA 559th Regiment moved on C Company near

Troops of the British 29th Brigade taken prisoner by the CPVA. (Photo PLA Daily)

Route 5Y and B Company on the Glosters' right flank. The Chinese penetrated the high ground of C Company's position commanding the mortars and battalion HQ in the valley beyond. Colonel Carne responded by pulling in the troops from the valley and C Company west over Route 5Y to positions between A and D companies in the Hill 235 area. This would leave Major Denis Harding's B Company isolated on the Glosters' right flank, but Carne believed it safer to leave the company where it was until daylight. This was not to be.

Instead of pursuing C Company or advancing down the valley where much of the 1/Glosters ammunition, food and general supplies had been abandoned, the CPVA turned all its attention to B Company on Hill 314. Wave upon wave of CPVA troops smashed into the company's perimeter, but in spite of inflicting major casualties on the Glosters—and suffering enormous losses themselves—they were unable to overrun the British position. As dawn broke, only fifteen unwounded members of B Company held out.

The CPVA now changed tactics. While maintaining pressure all around the B Company perimeter, a concentration of Chinese troops penetrated a platoon fire position, thereby breaching company defences. With this development, what was left of the company broke off the engagement to stumble down a path on the southern wooded slopes of the hill. Only twenty men survived the gauntlet and made it back to the main body of the battalion at Hill 235.

To the north-east of the developing 1/Glosters disaster, elements of the CPVA 188th Division swept down Route 11 to conduct a simultaneous frontal attack on 1/RUR and 1/RNF. By committing all their manpower to the front, the two battalions exposed their vulnerability to a flanking attack out of the 4-mile gap created between 1/RNF and the 1/Glosters when the latter withdrew to Hill 235.

By 7.30 a.m. that morning—24 April—Brigadier Brodie had despatched a hastily thrown-together task force, commanded by Filipino Lieutenant Colonel Dionisio Ojeda, comprising infantry, six Centurion tanks from 8/RIH and four Chaffee light tanks from 10/BCT, to clear Route 5Y and reinforce the Glosters. By mid-morning, however, conditions forced Brodie to change the operational nature of the mission. 10/BCT was to establish a blocking position at a pass 2 miles south of Hill 235 and only tanks would continue to the Glosters. But after a short distance a narrowing of the road into a gorge prevented the large Centurions from going any farther, thereby leaving the four Chaffees to complete the mission. By this time, Brodie had also given Colonel Carne the option of fighting his way to safety and linking up with the Filipinos at their blocking position.

As the crawling Chaffee column reached the small hamlet of Kwangsuwŏn shortly after 3 p.m., the three leading Chaffees, smothered in infantry and with open hatches, entered a narrow gorge flanked by high hills on either side of the track. The CPVA initiated their ambush with mortars and machine-gun fire. The first mortar bomb dropped through the driver's hatch of the first tank, while machine-gun fire cleared the hull of Filipinos. The 'cooking' Chaffee slewed to the left and blocked the track. A Centurion was brought forward to clear the route, but the lack of manoeuvrability in the confined space

An American M24 Chaffee light tank captured by the CPVA in Korea, Military Museum of the Chinese People's Revolution, Beijing, China. (Photo Morio)

made this virtually impossible. Meanwhile the rest of the column had gone ahead where, upon rounding a bend in the track, they were ambushed by two CPVA battalions. There was little chance of surviving such an onslaught.

Commander of the Centurion tanks, Major Henry Huth, informed brigade HQ that the road was blocked, and was given permission to withdraw. Huth understood this authority to include 10/BCT. It was apparent that Brodie had only consulted Soule after the event, but despite being fully aware of the Glosters' dire situation, allowed 10/BCT to continue to withdraw to the rear.

3. LAST STAND

'The army must become one with the people so that they see it as their own army. Such an army will be invincible.'

Mao Zedong

Late morning on 24 April 1951 saw a handful of Glosters survivors, who had escaped their captors the previous day when the battalion supply point was overrun, report that the Chinese had significantly strengthened their position in the gap, and that an estimated regiment-strong concentration was holding the high ground at Hill 675, just over 2 miles east of Hill 235. In view of this, US 3rd Division commander Major General Robert H. Soule informed Brodie that the BUNC could not be committed to action without his approval. Strangely, Soule did not question Brodie's decision to hold the Filipino 10/BCT short of the 1/Glosters beleaguered position. Instead, Soule planned to relieve the Glosters

Painting of the US 65th Infantry Regiment's bayonet charge against a Chinese division during the Korean War. (Dominic D'Andrea, commissioned by the National Guard Heritage Foundation)

and clear the Chinese from Hill 675 by employing a force made up of the 1st and 3rd battalions, US 65th Infantry Regiment (US 1/65th and US 3/65th), most of the US 64th Tank Battalion and the US 10th Field Artillery Battalion (FAB) to fight its way to Solma-ri. 10/BCT would hold its position until the relief force passed through, then follow behind.

Controversy still surrounds the timing of the attack, centred on why the fateful decision was made to only attack the next day. It is argued by some that Brodie's quintessentially British manner of understating a crisis led Soule to wrongly understand that the Glosters would survive the night. By describing the situation on Hill 235 as 'A bit sticky; things are pretty sticky down there,' the gravity of the situation was not put across and the relief attack put off for early the following morning.[*] There is also an argument that Brodie had been totally clear in his assurance to division that, in spite of overnight reverses, the Glosters could hold out another night until relieved.[†]

In a mid-afternoon visit to divisional HQ, generals Milburn (US I Corps), Van Fleet (US Eighth Army) and Ridgway (Commander-in-Chief UN Command) questioned why the Glosters' situation was not being addressed immediately. Soule explained his understanding of the current position on Hill 235, while detailing his plans for a relief mission at 6.30 a.m. the next day. The senior commanders accepted Soule's grasp of the situation and left.

It would only be upon his return to divisional HQ at 9 p.m., after visiting the US 7th Infantry, that General Soule learned of the withdrawal of the 10/BCT. However, he again accepted Brodie's explanation and assurance that the Glosters were set up to last another night. But by this time the Glosters were down to 350 combat-fit men.

Having recovered a small quantity of ammunition, food and other supplies from the abandoned battalion supply point, Colonel Carne, while not requesting a withdrawal, apprised Brodie of his uncertainty that his battalion could hold out against the Chinese much longer. In response, Brodie conveyed division orders that Carne had to hold his position until relief arrived in the morning.

During a lull in the CPVA assault, while the Chinese tightened their grip around the Glosters, Carne elected to make his stand on the knife-edge crest of Hill 235, where the hill dropped off steeply to the north-west and south-east. Under cover of darkness, he repositioned his men: A Company on the north-west and west, the remnants of B Company and C Company on the south and south-east and D Company on the north and north-east. Unbeknown to Carne, perhaps fortunately so, over the preceding twelve hours the CPVA LXIV Corps had forced the Glosters' left flank at Korangp'o-ri. While the 192nd Division, CPVA LXIV Corps, attacked across the ROKA 1st Division front, the CPVA 190th Division had penetrated the boundary between the ROKA 11th and 12th regiments. On the ROKA 12th Regiment's right flank, the 189th Division, CPVA LXIII Corps, forced the gap between the South Koreans and the Glosters on Hill 235.

---

* S.P. MacKenzie, *The Imjin and Kapyong Battle, Korea, 1951* (Indiana University Press, Bloomington, 2013).
† Billy C. Mossman, *Ebb and Flow, November 1950–July 1951* (Center of Military History, United States Army, Washington, 1990).

Shortly after Carne had disposed his men on Hill 235, at around 10 p.m. the CPVA attacked up the gentler north-western and south-eastern slopes. Major Harding's B Company and Captain Frank Wisbey's C Troop, 170 Mortar Battery, faced successive waves of Chinese, but the Glosters were able to withstand the assault by sheer volume of machine-gun fire. Just below the crest, A Company—Captain Donald Allman and seventeen men—was only just able to hold on.

Several hours later, the reinforced CPVA returned. This time, accurate fire from the 45th Field Regiment's 25-pounders stopped the enemy from breaching the Glosters' perimeter. However, A, B and C companies, with a portion of D Company within the field of fire, gave their all to survive.

At first light—25 April—an enemy attack from the north-west carried the Hill 235 crest. But with severely depleted numbers, the group of CPVA soldiers were forced off by a small but very determined Gloster counterattack. Even as the sun rose, the CPVA did not break off their attack, assembling troops to take on the north-western slopes. Responding to a request from Carne, a flight of F-80 Shooting Stars virtually annihilated the massed Chinese troops.

At the same time, the CPVA 187th and 188th divisions had moved so far down both the 1/Glosters' flanks, that the Chinese directed small-arms and mortar fire on the US

British Ordnance QF 25-pounder gun mounted on its firing platform. The gun was the British Army's primary artillery field piece of the Second World War and well into the 1960s. (Photo Gerry van Tonder)

1/65 and US 3/65th, the BUNC, the Philippine 10BCT, the British 45th Field Artillery, and the 29th British command post. Elements of the CPVA 188th, having descended Hill 675, cut Route 11 behind 1/RNF and 1/RUR.

In the brigade command post tent, a meeting had been scheduled for 4 a.m. to assess the latest situation and to make critical and immediate brigade decisions. Commander of the Puerto Rican 65th Infantry Regiment, US Army (attached US 3rd Division), Colonel William Harris, had been ordered to attend by General Soule with a view to providing a second task force to relieve the Glosters.

While waiting for Brodie, brigade chief engineer Major Anthony Younger, and Centurion commander Major Huth were told by staff officer Major James Dunning that he could not rouse the brigadier as he had taken sleeping pills to ensure much-needed rest. Before their commander showed, Younger and Huth had discussed what could be done to assist 1/RNF and 1/RUR come daylight. The two officers believed that a phased withdrawal of the two battalions under Centurion cover fire was required, as the CPVA were rapidly moving in behind their positions on Route 11 some 6 miles north. With only the weakened BUNC on hand for a rearguard, Younger indicated that his men would be tasked to hold a hill feature halfway to Hill 398.

Events were now extremely fluid, negating the luxury of time in which to make life-saving decisions, and even when decisions were made, the speed of the collapse of the US I Corps line meant that nothing was set in stone. When a sluggish Brodie eventually

The Centurion was the primary British main battle tank of the post-Second World War period. It first entered combat with the British Army in the Korean War in 1950, in support of the UN forces. (Photo Gerry van Tonder)

joined the meeting, a signal had already been received from General Milburn at US I Corps HQ stating that the whole corps was to withdraw south to Line Delta. Brodie endorsed the plan to relieve 1/RNF and 1/RUR, but had yet to offer a rescue of the Glosters.

General Soule's prime concern had, within a few hours, switched to retaining control of his division's main supply route, Route 33, as his line of retreat to Ŭijŏngbu. While his plans to employ the US 65th in an effort to save the Glosters offered hope, the hours of darkness of 24/25 April irrevocably changed the complexion of the situation in his eastern sector.

During a lull in the fighting the previous afternoon, the US 1/7th, at the time astride Route 33 on the US 3rd Division's right, had no difficulty in replacing the US 3/65 at the centre of the regiment, bringing the latter closer to the 29th British to prepare for the mission to relieve the Glosters. However, between 8 p.m. and midnight, two regiments of the CPVA 29th Division crossed the Hant'an River to attack all three battalions of the US 65th Regiment. The US 2/65th position was hardest hit, forcing a piecemeal withdrawal to regroup 4 miles south of Line Kansas, leaving the US 1/65th and 3/65th to hold the line for the night under intense enemy pressure.

To the east of the US I Corps sector, elements of the CPVA 29th Division and the CPVA 81st and 179th divisions fell on the US 25th Division with renewed impetus. As his 24th and 27th regiments buckled, division commander General Bradley pulled the two units back a mile south, but only to have the Chinese tail the move. On the corps' right flank, after again routing the ROKA 6th Division, the CPVA 60th Division slammed into the US 24th Division's 19th and 21st regiments. With the latter bending its line to protect its flank, and the existing gap created by the ROKA 6th Division, the rear divisional and corps echelons were now wide open to enemy attack.

At 5 a.m.—25 April—General Milburn issued orders for the withdrawal of US I Corps to Line Delta, running east–west between 4 and 12 miles south. The US 24th and 25th divisions would start to withdraw at 8 a.m., but the US 3rd and ROKA 1st divisions were not to withdraw before the surrounded Glosters were rescued. For General Soule, there was therefore no longer a need for the US 3rd Division to hold their position on Line Kansas, and so cancelled the US 65th's mission to relieve the Glosters that had been scheduled for 6.30 a.m. It was left to Brodie to radio Colonel Carne to give him the bad news which would effectively seal the Glosters' fate. At 6.10 a.m., Carne was informed that they were completely surrounded with no option to withdraw, but to continue to fight the Chinese onslaught.

Of immediate concern to Soule was the threat to Route 33 posed by the CPVA 189th Division. Anticipating the Chinese route of advance, Soule deployed the US 1/65th and 2/6th, 10/BCT and the US 3rd Reconnaissance Company in a blocking position. The US 3/65th would remain in position to the west of the 29th British to cover the withdrawal of 1/RNF and 1/RUR. In support of this cover, Brodie positioned the Belgians astride Route 11 just to the north of the brigade command post. Of all divisional manpower, including reserves, all that remained available to Soule to form a force to rescue the Glosters,

US 155-mm self-propelled gun in action in Korea. (Photo US Signals Corps)

were the US 64th Tank Battalion and the US 65th Infantry's tank company. Accordingly, he assigned the task and the assets to Brodie and Harris.

By 8 a.m., Brodie and Harris were still deliberating the content and method of the rescue mission. British Centurion tank commander Major Huth, having failed to reach the Glosters the previous day as his tanks were too large, convinced Brodie that only light tanks could be employed. A decision was thus reached to employ a platoon of tanks from Captain Claude Smith's US 65th Infantry tank company. Harris was not prepared to commit the whole company, but gave an assurance that there would be a follow-up if required. At 9 a.m., Captain Smith, less one tank under repair, started up Route 5Y in the direction of Hill 235.

By this time, close-quarter fighting characterized the situation atop Hill 235. Reduced to thirty able-bodied men, and all officers either dead or wounded, A Company, 1/Glosters, was pushed off its elevated position on the hill. The arrival of the battalion adjutant, Captain Anthony Farrar-Hockley, re-instilled morale and determination in the men, to the extent that they successfully answered his call to recover their commanding position.*

---

* Awarded the DSO, exceptional for a relatively junior rank, Farrar-Hockley would end an illustrious military career in the British army in 1982 as commander-in-chief of NATO Allied Forces, Northern Europe, with the rank and title of General Sir Anthony Heritage Farrar-Hockley, GBE, KCB, DSO and Bar, MC.

All the while, the British 25-pounders and USAF Shooting Stars continued to shoot up Chinese troop concentrations, but this support brought little or no respite. As with all the Glosters fighting to the death, A Company was now down to three rounds per rifle, two magazines for the Brens and a total of seven grenades. Officer commanding D Company, Captain Michael Harvey, reported that his men now had insufficient ammunition to withstand another Chinese attack.

To avoid envelopment themselves, the British 45th Field Regiment started to withdraw with the other British units, ending their support of the Glosters. All Brodie could now offer Carne was a suggestion that he break down what remained of his battalion into smaller groups to independently withdraw to the south west to junction with the ROKA 1st Division. South Korean commander General Kang had assembled a force comprising the 2nd Battalion, ROKA 12th Regiment, and two attached tank platoons of C Company, US 73rd Tank Battalion, to move up the small Nullori River to restore his right flank and from there attempt contact with the Glosters. Following what would be his last radio communication with Carne, Brodie ordered 1/RUR and 1/RNF to withdraw over Route 11 through the BUNC. Once these two battalions were joined by 1/Glosters,

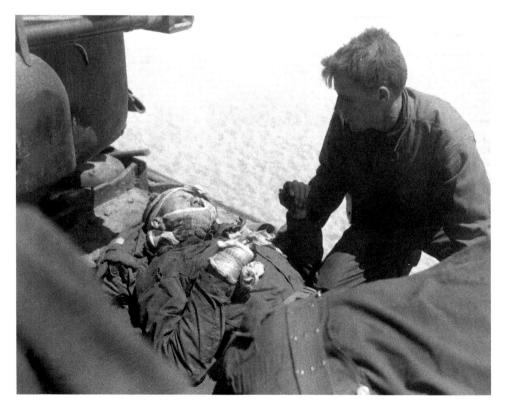

Crew members of the US 89th Tank Battalion render first aid to a soldier wounded in fighting against CPVA forces north-east of Seoul, 1951. (Photo Pfc. Charles Fabiszak)

Brodie would move his brigade south to Line Delta. However, considering the untenable and extremely dangerous positions in which the three British battalions were embroiled, Brodie's plan certainly exceeded the boundaries of rational optimism.

Around 10 a.m., while parties from A Company were the first to descend Hill 235, the US 65th tank platoon on Route 5Y was engaged by the CPVA well short of the Glosters. In the firefight, the tanks spent most of their ammunition and withdrew to their company's position, where Colonel Harris decided that no further attempts would be made.

As the Glosters staggered off Hill 235, the CPVA broke off their attack to concentrate on herding the British troops in the valley into larger groups by directing their fire to the sides. It was clear that the Chinese wanted prisoners to exploit in their propaganda. In what was left of A Company, Farrar-Hockley ordered the removal and disposal of rifle working parts before surrendering. Other officers followed suit, sparking accusations at some for not fighting hard enough.

Having escaped Hill 235 in a loop to the north-west and then southward, Captain Harvey led the remaining few officers and eighty-one soldiers of D Company in its break for freedom. Joined by eleven Vickers machine-gunners, Harvey was confident that fewer enemy forces would be encountered along the indirect route.

Now in the ROKA 1st Division sector, Harvey crossed the Nullori River as he headed south into a narrow canyon in the direction of the South Koreans. Suddenly, the Glosters came under heavy machine-gun fire from both sides as elements of the CPVA 192nd Division sprang their ambush. As each soldier tried desperately to avoid getting shot and to get out of the killing zone, the Glosters suffered another forty killed or taken prisoner.

Around midday, as what was left of D Company emerged from a bend in the valley, a troop of tanks from C Company, US 73rd Tank Battalion, opened fire on the Glosters with machine guns, wounding six. The British had been mistaken for the enemy as no one expected friendly troops to come from that direction. Realizing the error, the American tanks set out to bring the Glosters into safety. All that remained of D Company was Captain Harvey, plus three officers and thirty-six other ranks.

Over a period of four days from 22–25 April 1951, the 1st Battalion, the Gloucestershire Regiment, ceased to exist as a combat unit of the Korean War. Left to virtually fend for themselves against impossible odds without resupply, what would soon become known as the 'Glorious Glosters' suffered 580 casualties: 58 killed in action and a staggering 522 taken prisoner. A further 27 would die in captivity. But the trauma of 25 April was not yet over for the 29th British.

To avoid the CPVA that were swarming down on Route 11 from their Hill 675 stronghold, the able-bodied infantrymen of 1/RUR and 1/RNF, after passing through the Belgians, turned east off the road to make their way south over open country. Eight Centurion tanks loaded with 200 wounded, however, had no other alternative but to fight their way out. Heavy enemy machine-gun fire killed most of the wounded tied to the sides and backs of the British tanks. Six tanks were lost. As the brigade cleared, US3/65th engaged the pursuing CPVA at their blocking position, before breaking off and following the British.

Glosters survivors attend roll call after the Hill 235 disaster.

The 1st Battalion, the Royal Northumberland Fusiliers, lost twenty-two killed and fifty-six wounded. Included was the battalion commander, Lieutenant-Colonel Kingsley Foster, who died when his jeep was hit by CPVA mortar fire. Of the 1st Battalion, the Royal Ulster Regiment, 208 were killed or missing in action.

AMERICAN PRESIDENTIAL CITATION
Headquarters, Eighth United States Army Korea (EUSAK)
Office of the Commanding General
General Orders Number 286, 8 May 1951

BATTLE HONORS
By direction of the President, under the provisions of Executive Order 9396(Sec 1, WD Bul. 22.1943), superseding Executive Order 9075 (Sec.III, WD Bul.II, 1942) and pursuant in authority in AR 260-15, the following units are cited as public evidence of deserved honor and distinction. The citation reads as follows:

The 1ST BATTALION GLOUCESTERSHIRE REGIMENT, BRITISH ARMY and TROOP C, 170TH INDEPENDENT MORTAR BATTERY, ROYAL ARTILLERY, attached, are cited for exceptionally outstanding performance of duty and extraordinary heroism in action against the armed enemy near Solma-ri, Korea on the 23rd, 24th and 25th of April, 1951.

The 1st BATTALION and TROOP C were defending a very critical sector of the battle front during a determined attack by the enemy. The defending units were overwhelmingly outnumbered. The 83rd Chinese Communist Army drove the full force of its savage assault at the positions held by the 1st BATTALION, GLOUCESTERSHIRE REGIMENT and attached unit. The route of supply ran Southeast from the battalion between two hills. The hills dominated the surrounding terrain northwest to the Imjin River.

Enemy pressure built up on the battalion front during the day 23 April. On 24 April the weight of the attack had driven the right flank of the battalion back. The pressure grew heavier and heavier and the battalion and attached unit were forced into a perimeter defence on Hill 235. During the night, heavy enemy forces had by-passed the staunch defenders and closed all avenues of escape. The courageous soldiers of the battalion and attached unit were holding the critical route selected by the enemy for one column of the general offensive designed to encircle and destroy 1st Corps. These gallant soldiers would not retreat.

As they were compressed tighter and tighter in their perimeter defence, they called for close-in air strikes to assist in holding firm. Completely surrounded by tremendous numbers, these indomitable, resolute, and tenacious soldiers fought back with unsurpassed fortitude and courage. As ammunition ran low and the advancing hordes moved closer and closer, these splendid soldiers fought back viciously to prevent the enemy from overrunning the position and moving rapidly to the south. Their heroic stand provided the critically needed time to regroup other 1st Corps units and block the southern advance of the enemy.

Time and again efforts were made to reach the battalion, but the enemy strength blocked each effort. Without thought of defeat or surrender, this heroic force demonstrated superb battlefield courage and discipline. Every yard of ground they surrendered was covered with enemy dead until the last gallant soldier of the fighting battalion was over-powered by the final surge of the enemy masses.

The 1st BATTALION, GLOUCESTERSHIRE REGIMENT and TROOP C, 170th INDEPENDENT MORTAR BATTERY displayed such gallantry, determination, and esprit de corps in accomplishing their mission under extremely difficult and hazardous conditions as to set them apart and above other units participating in the same battle. Their sustained brilliance in battle, their resoluteness, and extraordinary heroism are in keeping with the finest traditions of the renowned military forces of the British Commonwealth, and reflect unsurpassed credit on these courageous soldiers and their homeland.

By Command of Lieutenant General Van Fleet.

British Foreign Secretary Philip Hammond pays his respects at Gloster Hill Memorial Park at Paju, Gyeonggi-do, 2015. The memorial to the Gloucestershire Regiment and C Troop, 170th Mortar Battery, Royal Artillery, stands at the foot of Gloster Hill, the initial location of the Gloucestershire Regiment's HQ during the battle at Imjin River. (Photo Commonwealth and Foreign Office)

Sabre 619 undergoing an engine change at Suwŏn airbase. K-55. (Robin Anderson)

4. DEFEAT TO VICTORY

'When American boys are being killed by Chinese armies, and Peking announces that they are fighting the United States and trying to destroy American forces we might as well have a declared war.'

Republican senator and presidential hopeful Robert A. Taft, January 1951

On 13 April 1951, it was announced that the newly activated 28th Commonwealth Infantry Brigade (Commonwealth 28th) would be replacing the 27th British Commonwealth Brigade as an overall restructuring of British and Commonwealth forces in the Korean theatre. In July that year, all such units would be combined under the command of the 1st Commonwealth Division. As part of the exercise, the 1/Argylls and 1/Middlesex would be relieved by the 1st Battalion, the King's Own Scottish Borderers (1/KOSB) and the 1st Battalion, the King's Shropshire Light Infantry (1/KSLI). The Commonwealth 28th would be commanded by Brigadier George Taylor DSO and Bar, a Second World War battle commander in the North-West Europe theatre.

Commonwealth troops in a rare jovial mood with captured North Korean posters. (Photo Alan Lambert)

By 16 April, the 27th British, now commanded by Brigadier Brian Arthur Burke, had advanced to Line Utah, at which point the brigade was to be relieved by the 19th Regiment, ROKA 6th Division (ROKA 19th). At the time, the South Korean division was on the brigade's right flank. The following day, the brigade was transported the 22 miles to Kap'yŏng into US IX Corps reserve, where the 1/Middlesex, 2/PPCLI and 3/RAR were placed on three hours' notice to any one of three fronts: the ROKA 6th Division (north), the US 1st Marine Division (north-east) and the US 24th Division (north-west).

In the afternoon of 22 April, while the ROKA 6th Division was still moving north, commander General Chang Do-yong was informed that aerial reconnaissance had observed large numbers of CPVA troops heading in his direction. Chang immediately called a halt, positioning his 19th Regiment (ROKA 19th) to the left and 2nd Regiment (ROKA 2nd) the right. From reserve, the 7th Regiment (ROKA 7th) fell in behind the ROKA 2nd.

Positioned in a strong, textbook defensive position on commanding high ground, the US 1st Marine Division (US IX Corps) was positioned on his right flank and the US 24th Division (US I Corps) on his left. In support were the 105-mm howitzers of the ROKA 27th FAB, the 25-pounders of the New Zealand 16th Field Regiment, Royal New Zealand Artillery (NZ 16th)—who had not gone into reserve with the rest of the British 27th—and the 4.2-inch mortars of C Company, US 2nd Chemical Mortar Battalion. From the US IX Corps, General Hoge positioned the US 92nd Armored FAB (155-mm self-propelled guns), the US 987th Armored FAB (105-mm howitzers) and the US 2nd Rocket FAB in placements of support should the South Koreans require it.

However, what could not be taken into account was the mental state of Chang's troops. Even before the arrival of the CPVA, a mortal fear of the Chinese among frontline South Koreans left forward defensive positions either incomplete or inadequate. Officers and NCOs lacked the competence, and in many instances the desire, to remedy the dangerous situation.

An hour after sunset, the CPVA 179th Regiment and units of the CPVA 120th Division had little difficulty pushing through gaps in the South Korean defences. Hitting the ROKA 2nd left flank first, the Chinese then moved behind the ROKA 2nd and the ROKA 19th. The result was immediate panic and flight, as the ROKA 7th and the ROKA 27th FAB joined the other two infantry regiments in disorganized retreat, abandoning weaponry, vehicles and equipment. In the ensuing chaos, the US IX Corps supporting elements were left fully exposed, forcing the US 987th Armored FAB to abandon half its 105-mm howitzers, while the US 2nd Rocket FAB and C Company, US 2nd Chemical Mortar Battalion, lost all of their hardware and equipment.

In the early hours of 23 April, the NZ 16th reported that the ROKA 19th had 'withdrawn' to Line Kansas and that elements of the US 1st Marine Division on the South Koreans' right flank were under attack. Ordered to withdraw, by 6.10 a.m. the NZ 16th was clear of the ROKA 19th area. Joined by 1/Middlesex for protection, the New Zealanders, less one battery, resumed their position with the ROKA 6th Division.

At 2.15 p.m., US IX Corps HQ ordered Brigadier Burke to occupy blocking positions east of Kap'yŏng: 3/RAR on Hill 504 and 2/PPCLI on Hill 677. Brigade HQ and 1/Argylls would remain in the old assembly area to the north of the town. Later that afternoon,

A 25-pounder crew from the 16 Field Regiment, Royal New Zealand Artillery, in action against the CPVA. (Photo Australian War Memorial)

two companies of the US 2nd Chemical Mortar Battalion, each with twelve 4.2-inch mortars, were attached to brigade HQ, while 3/RAR and 2/PPCLI were given one company each.

At around 8 p.m., news came in that the ROKA 19th were now again under attack on Line Kansas. As fleeing South Korean troops passed through the NZ 16th position, the New Zealanders and 1/Middlesex were pulled back into brigade HQ area, arriving there at 11 p.m. At this time, a battery of American 105-mm self-propelled guns and a battery from US 213 FAB were attached to the British brigade.

With landline communications damaged by tank movement, the British 27th had to rely on unreliable radio contact. At 1.40 a.m.—24 April— Lieutenant-Colonel Bruce Ferguson, commanding 3/RAR, radioed brigade HQ from the 1/Middlesex rear link to report that two battles were in progress in his area: one with D Company in front of Hill 504 and one around battalion HQ.

The critical point was in battalion HQ area where enemy troops had intermingled with South Korean vehicles and personnel passing through. Confused fighting broke out as HQ staff, the Assault Pioneer Platoon and the Anti-tank and Mortar platoons attempted to engage the Chinese infiltrators. Eventually, the Australians were able to stop the South Koreans from leaving the HQ area, employing them to challenge the enemy. General Chang informed US IX Corps that he had been able to muster between 4,000 and 5,000 men, about half the South Korean division's strength.

After routing the ROKA 19th Regiment, the CPVA 60th Division had veered to the right to strike at the US 24th Division, leaving the CPVA 118th Division to speed down the Kap'yŏng valley where its CPVA 354th Regiment had reached 3/RAR at 10 p.m. At the entrance to the valley, the Chinese regiment had split and advanced on either side of a low north–south ridge, on which B Company, 3/RAR and 1st Platoon, A Company, US 72nd Tank Battalion were positioned. The other three 3/RAR companies were to the east on and around Hill 504.

Come daylight, there was no let-up in the Chinese assault on the 3/RAR front, but the Australians held their position and were able to clear the HQ area by mid-morning. There was, however, concern about their right flank and CPVA envelopment from the rear. B Company was ordered to withdraw to C Company's position, with 1st Platoon, A Company, US 72nd Tank Battalion carrying the wounded, ammunition and medical supplies. 2nd Platoon tanks were deployed at the Kap'yŏng ford to cover the withdrawal, while 4th Platoon set up a blocking position on the road between B Company on the ridge and Hill 504.

4th Platoon immediately came under enemy fire, during which four crewmen were wounded, including two tank commanders. The platoon commander was fatally wounded.

Troops of a 3rd Battalion, Royal Australian Regiment outpost look on as supporting artillery bombards CPVA positions. (Photo Australian War Memorial)

First Lieutenant Kenneth W. Koch, commander of the tank company, reorganized the crippled platoon under the leadership of a sergeant and ordered him to join 2nd Platoon covering the north-west. The CPVA 354th Regiment now attacked across the whole front, with elements reaching 1/Middlesex farther south.

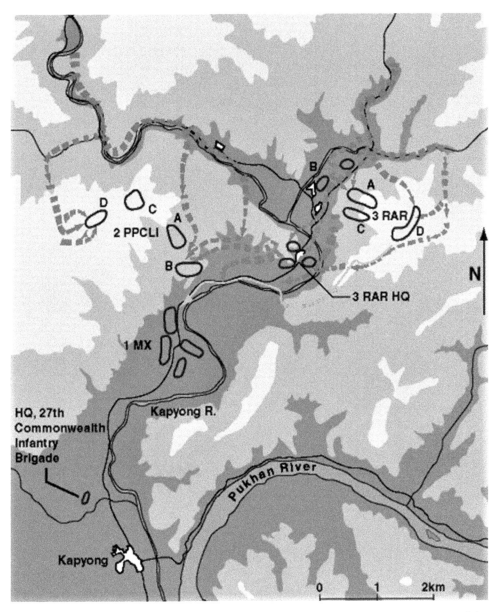

The situation on the Kapyong River towards the end of April 1951, showing the positions of the 2nd Battalion, Princess Patricia's Canadian Light Infantry (2/PPCLI), the 3rd Battalion, Royal Australian Regiment (3/RAR) and the 1st Battalion, Middlesex Regiment (1/MX). (Wikipedia)

At 11 a.m., Brigadier Burke ordered 3/RAR to withdraw south to the 1/Middlesex lines. But with the CPVA established astride the road between the two positions, Colonel Ferguson ordered his battalion to move along high ground to the east. Major B.S. O'Dowd, commanding A Company, 3/RAR, was tasked with directing the withdrawal through D Company. Laying down a smokescreen, the move began along a ridgeline south-west to the river flat just south of the 1/Middlesex forward companies.

It would take the Australians seven hours to complete their withdrawal, during which time US Marine Corsairs accidentally dropped napalm on the rearguard D Company position on Hill 504, killing one and wounding three.

The casualties suffered by the Australian battalion in the Kap'yŏng fight numbered twenty-two killed, six dying of wounds, sixty-three wounded and seven missing, presumed killed.

U.N. AIRCRAFT MAY BOMB MANCHURIA

An American delegation spokesman said at Lake Success there was no doubt that if the Chinese Communists launched "massive air attacks" in Korea, United Nations aircraft would bomb bases beyond the Korean border. The spokesman said that the matter had been discussed in Washington by Mr. Dean Rusk, American Under-Secretary of State, and representatives of the fourteen Powers with military forces in Korea. He denied a Press report that these representatives had given their agreement to the bombing of Chinese bases.

Canadian View
The Canadian Minister for External Affairs, Mr. Lester Pearson, told the Canadian House of Commons yesterday that Canada and other countries with troops in Korea should be consulted before any action to bomb Chinese air bases in Manchuria was taken. He also said that such action might be necessary without consultation in cases where Chinese planes were chased back to their bases. In such cases military necessity would decide the issue.

Derry Journal, Friday 27 April 1951

Out on a limb to the west of the Australians, the Second Battalion, Princess Patricia's Canadian Light Infantry (2/PPCLI), positioned on Hill 677 overlooking the Kap'yŏng River valley, came under attack by vastly superior numbers of the CPVA during the night of 24/25 April.

Commanded by Lieutenant-Colonel James R. Stone, the battalion was raised specifically for an eighteen-month tour of duty for which volunteers, particularly with

Troops of the Princess
Patricia's Canadian
Light Infantry, Korea.
(Photo NARA)

Second World War experience, were advertised. Untrained as a combat unit, the 'Patricias', as they were commonly referred to, arrived by US naval transport on 18 December 1950. After completing seven weeks of training, the 2/PPCLI was assigned to the 27th British, a part of the US IX Corps. Over the next two months, the Canadians engaged CPVA rear-guard positions as the corps advanced on the 38th Parallel, during which D Company sustained thirty-four casualties in nine hours of fighting at Hill 532.

With the collapse of the ROKA 6th Division in the night of 22/23 April, the 27th British received rushed orders to block the gap to the north of the Kap'yŏng River. 2/PPCLI was to establish blocking positions covering the northern and north-eastern brigade sector, centred on Hill 677.

From early on 23 April, reconnaissance patrols were conducted by Colonel Stone, together with the four company commanders and senior support and intelligence staff. Access to the hill was identified and company areas along its ridge lines defined.

At 6 p.m., 2/PPCLI was transported to the village of Tungmudae, from where the mile to Hill 677 was covered on foot. By 10 p.m., the companies were in position and digging in: D Company on the left flank on the northern approaches to Hill 677, C Company on the ridgeline in the centre, A Company on the right flank, and B Company to the north-east of the battalion's tactical HQ on the commanding southern slopes of Hill 677 overlooking Tungmudae. However, the terrain did not allow for an unbroken battalion line, resulting in gaps between company dispositions that would have to rely on artillery, mortar and machine-gun support to defend.

By 4 a.m.—24 April—the battalion tactical HQ was operational. Included at the position was the Mortar Platoon's 81-mm mortars, with 2,100 bombs, and twenty-four .30 and .50 Browning machine guns. Defence positions for support company and HQ personnel were established within the HQ perimeter that was laid out with trip-wire set with No. 36M Mk. I Mills grenades. By this time, 3/RAR on the Canadians' right flank had been under major attack for several hours from elements of the CPVA 118th Division, the sights and sounds unnerving many of the Patricias.

Out of concern that the Australians would not be able to hold Hill 504, Colonel Stone moved Major Vince Lilley's B Company several hundred yards eastward to facilitate a better view of the Kap'yŏng valley. As it transpired, Stone's forethought was well founded. By the time B Company had reached their objective by late morning, 3/RAR battalion HQ ordered its now isolated and embattled companies to conduct a fighting withdrawal.

CBC war correspondents Normand Eaves, holding the microphone, and Norman McBain, at the controls, interviewing a British officer, Korea, 1951. (Photo Paul E. Tomelin)

For the Canadians, the remaining hours of daylight were quiet, apart from Brigadier Burke's weak attempt at boosting the Patricias' morale by broadcasting a pep-talk from a loud-speaker-equipped Dakota C-47 flying over their position. However, the arrival of American reinforcements that afternoon in the 27th British sector provided much-needed encouragement.

On June 25, 1950 the forces of North Korea crossed the 38th Parallel into the Republic of Korea. This marked the beginning of hostilities which were to rage for three full years and more, throughout that country known to its people as the Land of the Morning Calm. The magnitude of the assault made it clear that this was a full-scale invasion.

This was the first open act of aggression since the establishment of the United Nations Organization and its actions were of great significance for its prestige and credibility—in fact for its very future. The invasion was declared a breach of the peace, and 16 member nations joined forces to resist the aggression.

Canada's contribution, exceeded only by that of the United States and Great Britain, demonstrated her willingness to uphold the United Nations ideals and to take up arms in support of peace and freedom. All told, 26,791 Canadians served in the Korean War and approximately 7,000 continued to serve in the theatre between the cease-fire and the end of 1955. The names of 516 Canadian dead are inscribed in the Korea Book of Remembrance.

Canadian participation in these hostilities marked a break with traditional policy. It was the beginning of a new era of involvement in world affairs which saw Canadian troops deployed around the world in truce teams, peace commissions and emergency forces. A new page in Canada's proud military history was written.

Veterans Affairs Canada, www.veterans.gc.ca/eng

The 5th Cavalry Regiment, US 1st Cavalry Division (US 5th Cavalry), was moved in to ensure that the town of Kap'yŏng did not fall to the CPVA. One battalion was deployed to the south-west of Hill 677 to protect the 2/PPCLI's left flank. Another took up a position across the Kap'yŏng River and south-east of 1/Middlesex. A replacement British battalion, the 1st Battalion, King's Own Scottish Borderers (1/KSOB), also arrived during the day to join 3/RAR at brigade HQ.

At around 9.30 p.m., having taken Hill 504 from the Australians, the 354th Regiment, CPVA 118th Division, veered to the west to capture the high ground dominated by Hill 677, initiating an attack on B Company, 2/PPCLI, with mortar and machine-gun fire. Half an hour later, his platoon in imminent danger of being overrun,

A US Marine Corps Vought F4U Corsair drops napalm, Imjin River. (Photo US Navy)

Lieutenant H. Ross received orders from Major Lilley to fix bayonets and fight their way onto the main company position. A Patricia described his own personal experience:

> Ross gave us the order to move out. Just as we jumped up Ross added that anyone with ammo left should cover the retreat of the wounded. I had three shells left so I dropped back down and fired them off. Just as I jumped up again, I fell over a Chinaman who was running up the side of the hill. He let fly and got me in the neck then ran into the end of my bayonet.*

While B Company fought desperately to prevent being overwhelmed, CPVA troops swung to the rear of the 2/PPCLI tactical HQ to envelop the Canadians. However, a curtain of fire from the Mortar Platoon's massed machine-guns poured down on the assailants, ensuring the integrity of the HQ perimeter. As the CPVA broke off their attack, effective heavy .50-calibre machine-gun fire was turned on enemy troops wading through the Kap'yŏng

---

* Brent Watson (2000), 'Recipe for Victory: The Fight for Hill 677 during the Battle of the Kap'yong River, 24–25 April 1951' in *Canadian Military History*: Vol. 9: Issue 2, Article 2.

River 600 yards away, their advance visible in the bright moonlight. At this time, brigade ordered elements of A Company, US 72nd Tank Battalion, to move on the rear of Hill 677 to disrupt the Chinese attack on the Canadians' HQ.

At 4 a.m.—25 April—10 Platoon, D Company, on the Canadians' left flank, came under attack from an estimated 200 CPVA. In the attack, the Chinese overran the 12 Platoon medium machine-gun section that was providing support to 10 Platoon, killing two Canadians and capturing two Vickers machine guns.

Running low on shells, the NZ 16th reduced the supporting rate of fire of their 25-pounders to two rounds a minute, defined as 'slow' and amounting to twenty-four rounds every thirty seconds dropping into the target area. Soon, however, this was further reduced to one round per gun a minute.

In the unrelenting enemy attack, 10 Platoon became isolated and 12 Platoon was overrun, forcing the latter to fall back on the D Company command post. In a desperate move, acting company commander Captain Walter Mills called for artillery fire directly on to his position. He assured HQ that his men were safely dug in below ground level. For twenty minutes air-burst shells caused havoc over D Company's position. Shrapnel and steel ball bearings flying in all directions tore through the CPVA troops, forcing the Chinese to break off contact. Exploiting the successful artillery bombardment, Mills signalled the New Zealand gunners to revert to shelling the sloping approaches to his position.

The Princess Patricia's Canadian Light Infantry, seen here training in England in 1942, retained their Second World War Vickers machine guns as support weapons in Korea. (Sergeant John S. Towers)

For the remaining hours of darkness, the Chinese launched successive attacks on D Company in their efforts to infiltrate battalion tactical HQ. But the Canadians, with help from the New Zealanders' guns, held the line, and as day dawned, the CPVA broke off their attack. In the whole engagement, the NZ 16th had fired more than 2,200 rounds.

After the Chinese withdrawal, 12 Platoon returned to its original position where the two Vickers machine guns were recovered, undamaged and still loaded. At the same time, B Company resumed occupation of its forward position.

The CPVA penetration of the Kap'yŏng Valley had resulted in the severance of the supply route from brigade HQ to the Canadians. Colonel Stone's urgent request for an airdrop of ammunition and supplies saw four C-119 Flying Boxcars successfully execute a drop on the Canadians position on Hill 677. The lull in the fighting also allowed for the evacuation of casualties by US Army helicopter. Early that afternoon, the track on the approaches to Hill 677 was declared clear of enemy forces and replenishment by vehicle commenced. The remaining dead and wounded could now also be trucked out. Miraculously, 2/PPCLI lost only ten killed and twenty-three wounded in its three-day fight against overwhelming odds to hold the line in defence of Kap'yŏng.

A US Air Force Fairchild C-119B Flying Boxcar on a supply drop near Chŏngju, Korea, 1951. (Photo USAF)

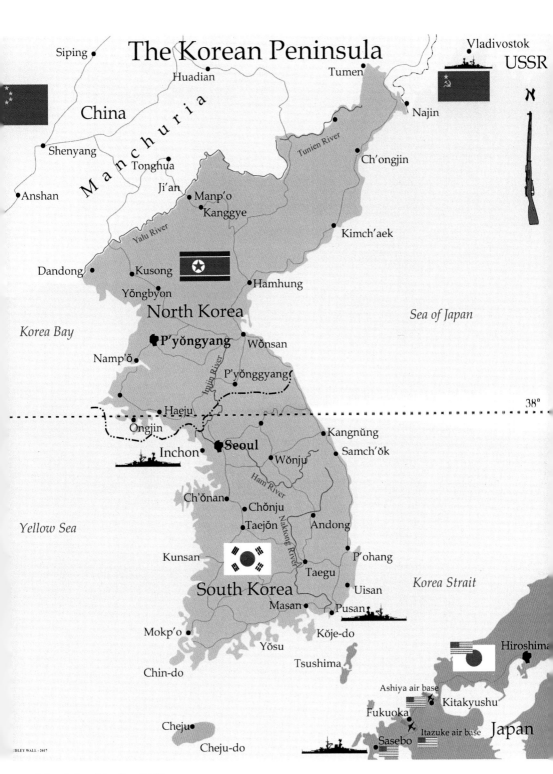

(Map Colonel Dudley Wall)

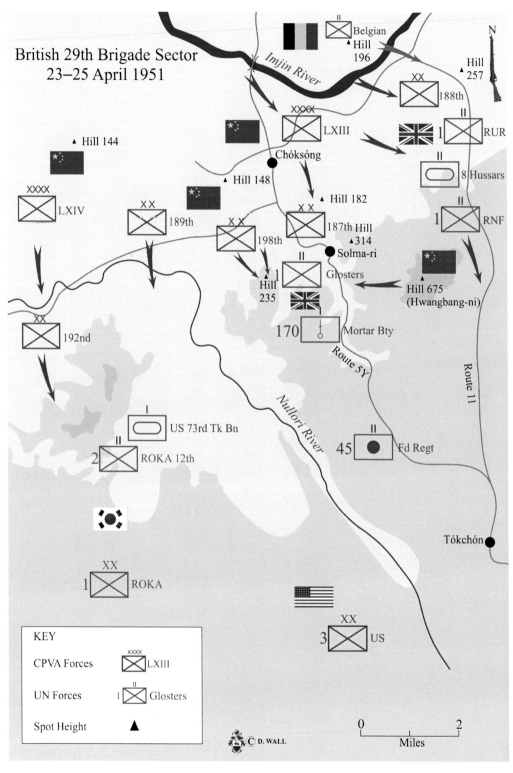

The British 29th Brigade sector, Battle of Imjin River, 23–25 April 1951. (Map Colonel
Dudley Wall)

Above and below: The Gloucestershire Regiment Victoria Cross commemorative plaques to Lieutenant-Colonel James Carne and Lieutenant Philip Curtis (posthumous), National Memorial Arboretum, Alrewas, England. (Photos Gerry van Tonder)

Badges of the Korean War

American and British badges of the Korean War period. (Colonel Dudley Wall collection)

Above: The British Centurion Mk. 3 main battle tank of the type employed by the 8th King's Royal Irish Hussars to successively cover the withdrawal of the 29th Brigade during the Battle of the Imjin River. (Photo Balcer)

Below: The ubiquitous T-35/85 medium tank, mainstay of communist armour during the Korean War. (Photo ProDiman)

Above: The heavy cruiser USS *St. Paul* (CA-73) at Naval Station Yokosuka, Japan. On 21 April 1952, four months after this photograph was taken, one of the cruiser's 8-inch gun turrets suffered a sudden powder fire, killing thirty sailors. (Photo US Navy)

Below: The battleship USS *Iowa* (BB-61) fires her 16-inch guns into North Korea in the summer of 1952. (US Navy)

Above: Royal Navy Hawker Sea Fury fighter-bombers such as this restored example, were deployed primarily as ground-attack aircraft, from the Royal Navy light-fleet carriers HMS *Glory*, HMS *Theseus*, HMS *Ocean*, and the Australian carrier HMAS *Sydney*. (Photo Dave Miller)

Below: A Douglas A-1D Skyraider AD-4 in US Navy livery. (Photo Tim Felce)

A South Korean soldier, showing his back, adopts a Taekwondo stance meant to intimidate his North Korean counterpart who is standing against the north–south divide, P'anmunjŏm, Demilitarized Zone. (Photo Sergeant Jack Braden)

Early in the afternoon, a brigade tank patrol reported little enemy activity. 1/Middlesex relieved a battalion of the US 5th Cavalry near Hill 507, their position being taken by 3/RAR. Reports from the Canadians of a CPVA concentration on Hill 865 and in the mist-shrouded valley to the north resulted in effective artillery fire and airstrikes on these positions. From 4 p.m. enemy pressure on the brigade front suddenly eased and no further attacks came in. Elements of the US 5th Cavalry continued to exploit the lull in fighting to retake Hill 504 lost by the Australians the day before. Before last light, a column of tanks, engineers and infantry set off on what turned out to be an unopposed patrol down the road to Ch'unch'ŏn.

At one minute after midnight—26 April—the title and command of the 27th British changed. Commander Brigadier Brian Burke DSO handed over to Brigadier George Taylor DSO, commanding officer of the 28th British Commonwealth Brigade. Before departing for Hong Kong, Burke 'presented the Brigade flag to Lieut Col I.B. Ferguson, CO 3 RAR, in token of the great comradeship enjoyed and for the high esteem which was held throughout the Brigade for the 3rd Bn, Royal Australian Regiment'.*

The 27th British with support from A Company, US 72nd Tank Battalion (on attachment from the US Eighth Army), had prevented superior numbers of CPVA forces from taking Kap'yŏng, earning an American Presidential Unit citation 'for extraordinary heroism and outstanding performance of combat duties in action against the armed enemy near Kapyong, Korea, on 24 and 25 April 1951'. The citation, contained in General Order No. 453 of 23 June 1951, reads in part:

> The 3rd Battalion, Royal Australian Regiment, moved to the right flank of the sector and took up defensive positions north of the Pukham [sic] River. The 2nd Battalion, Princess Patricia's Canadian Light Infantry, defended in the vicinity of Hill 677 on the left flank. Company A, 72nd Heavy Tank Battalion, supported all units to the full extent of its capacity and, in addition, kept the main roads open and assisted in evacuating the wounded.
>
> Troops from a retreating division passed through the sector which enabled enemy troops to infiltrate with the withdrawing forces. The enemy attacked savagely under the clamor of bugles and trumpets. The forward elements were completely surrounded going through the first day and into the second. Again and again the enemy threw waves of troops at the gallant defenders, and many times succeeded in penetrating the outer defences, but each time the courageous, indomitable, and determined soldiers repulsed the fanatical attacks.
>
> Ammunition ran low and there was no time for food. Critical supplies were dropped by air to the encircled troops, and they stood their ground in resolute defiance of the enemy. With serene and indefatigable persistence, the gallant

---

* *27th British Commonwealth Brigade War Diary January to April 1951* (The Australia War Memorial archives, Campbell).

soldiers held their defensive positions and took heavy tolls of the enemy. In some instances when the enemy penetrated the defences, the commanders directed friendly artillery fire on their own positions in repelling the thrusts. Toward the close of 25 April, the enemy breakthrough had been stopped. The seriousness of the breakthrough on the central front had been changed from defeat to victory by the gallant stand of these heroic and courageous soldiers. The 3rd Battalion, Royal Australian Regiment; 2nd Battalion, Princess Patricia's Canadian Light Infantry; and Company A, 72nd Heavy Tank Battalion, displayed such gallantry, determination, and esprit de corps in accomplishing their missions under extremely difficult and hazardous conditions as to set them apart and above other units participating in the campaign, and by their achievements they brought distinguished credit on themselves, their homelands, and all freedom-loving nations.

US Eighth Army commander, General Van Fleet, was now confident that he would be able to keep Seoul in UN hands. There was no doubt that the sacrifices of Imjin and the defence of Kap'yŏng by British and Commonwealth forces had done much to knock the wind out of the Chinese offensive. Tactically, the CPVA had lost three days and in terms of combat capability, an estimated 70,000 troops. Albeit that he had only been in command for two weeks, Van Fleet was adamant that there would be no retreat south of the Han River.

General James Van Fleet (first left) inspects troops of the 3rd Battalion, Royal Australian Regiment, after Kap'yŏng. (Photo Australian War Memorial)

General Milburn also capitalized on these events. He would still withdraw from Line Delta south to Line Golden, as he saw no tactical advantage in trying to defend the former without reconsolidating his US I Corps forces. However, the withdrawal would be phased and strictly controlled. Objective lines would be marked out between Delta and Golden, primarily to ensure that artillery would be in range to cover each such line being vacated. The moves would be executed in daylight hours so that any pursuing enemy forces would be visible and therefore open to artillery fire and airstrikes.

Following overnight attacks along his corps sector of Line Delta by elements of the KPA I Corps and the CPVA Nineteenth Army, in the morning of 26 April, Milburn initiated his phased withdrawal. The 11th Regiment, ROKA 1st Division, straddling Route 1 and the US 65th on the US 3rd's left flank, took the brunt of the attack. The CPVA forced a 5-mile gap between the ROKA 1st and 3rd divisions, but they did not press the advantage deeper. Milburn's next phase line lay just above the town of Ŭijŏngbu, ranging 2 to 5 miles south of Delta on an east–west axis.

Across the peninsula, the US IX and X corps would conform to retain an unbroken line. On Milburn's right flank, General Hoge was to order the ROKA 6th Division, US IX Corps, to withdraw to the US I Corps' new right flank. To Hoge's east, the 28th British would reoccupy the high ground positions previously held by 3/RAR and 2/PPCLI to the north of Kap'yŏng. On his corps' right flank, the US 1st Marine Division was to withdraw from Line Kansas to positions astride the Pukhan River, then eastward to the northern approaches to Ch'unch'ŏn, and then along the south bank of the Soyang River. To comply with the eastward chain reaction, General Almond, commander of US X Corps, would secure his left flank by pulling the US 2nd and 7th divisions back from the Hwach'ŏn Reservoir and the west front of the KPA salient in the Inje area. From this junction with the Marines, Almond's line would continue east along the Soyang River to south of Yanggu, and from there to the current position of the ROKA 5th Division south of Inje.

As a consequence of the major losses suffered by the CPVA LXIII Corps during the stand of 1/Glosters and the seemingly disjointed initial advance of the CPVA LXIV Corps in that sector, the CPVA Nineteenth Army command was forced to commit the CPVA LXV Corps in an attempt to restore the offensive in the west. For General Van Fleet there was a discernible reduction in the strength of the Chinese offensive across the peninsula, particularly in the central and eastern sectors. With only US I Corps under serious threat, Van Fleet sought to rationalize the trans-peninsular defence line to reflect the situation towards the end of April.

Dubbed 'No Name Line'—Van Fleet did not follow customary naming protocol—the new line incorporated Line Golden above Seoul before extending east to a point 5 miles north of the Pukhan's confluence with the Han River. From here, the line thrust sharply to the north-east, cutting routes 29 and 24 south of Ch'unch'ŏn and Inje respectively, before dropping off to the east coast a short distance north of Yangyang.

As night fell on 26 April, combined CPVA and KPA forces fell on each of the US I Corps divisions, with the exception of the US 24th on the corps' right flank. On the

US 25th Division front, the CPVA infiltrated a mile in between two companies of the US 27th Regiment, where they were checked by divisional reserves. Employing radar-directed bombing strikes and intensive ground fire, assisted by light from ship-fired flares, the Chinese were annihilated.

Typically, the enemy targeted South Korean units as experience had shown these to be weak points in the UN lines. The attack on the ROKA 1st Division, and the US 65th to the left of the US 3rd Division sector west of Ŭijŏngbu, was particularly severe. While airstrikes and artillery fire assisted the US 65th in holding its position, the Chinese forced the 15th Regiment, ROKA 1st Division, back 2 miles before the South Koreans dug in. Attacking south along the Route 1 corridor the 8th and 47th divisions, KPA I Corps, slammed into the ROKA 11th Regiment and the South Korean tank destroyer battalion to the east of Haengju. The North Koreans were eventually stopped by South Korean counterattacks backed by American tanks, but not before inflicting heavy casualties on the tank destroyer battalion.

At 6 a.m. on 27 April, the US 24th Division was transferred to the US I Corps command as General Milburn moved his units to the final interim phase line 1–7 miles above Line Golden. The previous day he had reinforced the US 3rd Division with the US 7th Cavalry, a fortuitous move as elements of the CPVA Nineteenth Army continued to apply pressure

A Korean People's Army command post.

on the ROKA 1st Division. It would be late afternoon before General Kang would be able to disengage his South Korean troops while still fighting, employing the ROKA 11th, 15th and 12th regiments to the front of the second phase line.

By first light on 28 April, Van Fleet was sufficiently confident of the UN forces' positions that he instructed his corps commanders to execute an 'active' defence of No Name Line, using artillery and armour assets to the full to accomplish this. This would translate to US I Corps forces digging in north of the Han River, considered by some of Van Fleet's staff to be a tactical error.

That morning, as US I Corps pulled back to Line Golden, North Korean troops were observed concentrating near Haengju, a village on the east bank of the Han River opposite the Kimp'o Airfield. Having moved from the Sea of Japan to a station just off of Inch'ŏn, the cruiser USS *Toledo* laid down an 8-inch barrage which, together with the massed fire of two artillery battalions, neutralized the threat. Apart from an unsuccessful enemy attack on the US 7th Cavalry south of Ŭijŏngbu, the rest of the day remained relatively quiet.

By early evening, the withdrawal to Line Golden and dispositioning of front units and reserves were complete. The US I Corps had six regiments on the line and another six in and on the outskirts of Seoul. To the south of the South Korean capital and the Han River, the 29th British and Turkish brigades were in place on the west and east flanks to avert potential enemy envelopment of Seoul.

There was now increasing evidence that the Chinese spring offensive, launched a week earlier, had lost its momentum and impetus. Information gleaned from captured Chinese attested to this, as American interdiction bombing of rear areas and airstrikes on forward units had prevented the forward movement of much-need artillery support. Confusion and a serious reduction in cohesion gave rise to the issuing of broad, often misleading orders. The fighting had exacted a major toll on political commissars at key levels in the command structure, damaging the very fabric on which the efficacy and success of Mao's peasant armies depended: motivation and discipline.

On 29 April, troops of the KPA 8th Division massed in preparation of another attack, this time on the US 25th Division, but heavy artillery fire and airstrikes that night stopped the North Koreans from even launching their attack. Patrols the next morning discovered around 1,000 dead North Korean troops at the site. The US I Corps front had become so quiet that patrols jumping off from Line Golden were moving unopposed as far as 6 miles north. The enemy had broken off contact and was withdrawing. Seoul was to remain in UN hands for the rest of the conflict.

The outloading of stocks of supplies and the 10,000 South Koreans operating the key port of Inch'ŏn was completed by 30 April. As the harbour was vacated, General Ridgway ordered General Van Fleet not to inflict any damage to the port such as when it had been abandoned in January: Inch'ŏn was to remain intact in the event that it might be needed again in the future, and should therefore also be protected by UN forces.

In military terms, especially when considering the sheer magnitude of operations, between 22 and 29 April US Army divisions sustained 1,914 casualties, including 314 dead.

An airstrike against a North Korean train, launched from USS *Bon Homme Richard*, October 1952. (Photo US Navy)

In the defence of Kap'yŏng, the Australians suffered 32 killed and 59 wounded, and the Canadians 10 killed and 23 wounded.

Comparative enemy casualty estimates, although varying between sources, verged on the catastrophic in comparison. A US Eighth Army HQ report for the period, taken only from ground unit daily situation reports, lists 13,300 known dead, an estimated 24,000 wounded and 246 POWs. The UN Command HQ in Tokyo placed the estimate at 75,000–80,000 casualties, including 50,000 in the fight for Seoul.

However, General Van Fleet warned against complacency. The enemy had sustained significant losses, but its numbers, particularly in the CPVA, were so large that their forces remained formidable. As of 1 May, enemy forces were estimated to number 542,000 Chinese and 197,000 North Korean troops. General Ridgway's US Eighth Army command staff estimated that around 300,000 enemy troops were poised to attack along his defences, particularly in the central sector.[*]

---

[*] Billy C. Mossman, *Ebb and Flow, November 1950–July 1951* (Center of Military History, United States Army, Washington, 1990).

5. CEASEFIRE

'There are not enough Chinamen in the world to stop a fully armed Marine regiment from going wherever they want to go.'

Brigadier General Lewis B. 'Chesty' Puller, USMC

The Chinese spring offensive, or Fifth Offensive, of April 1951, incorporating reconstituted North Korean units, proved to be pivotal in the Korean War. Inflicting enormous losses on the enemy, and with the British and Commonwealth brigades playing key roles, the US Eighth Army line across the Korean peninsula absorbed and repulsed what turned out to be the biggest enemy offensive of the conflict. The CPVA was no longer considered invincible, its strength and logistical support severely mauled. Away from the mass killing grounds, the word 'truce' was being spoken in secret. Essentially, the frontline would remain largely static, in a stalemate cycle of attack and counterattack that would ultimately force a truce in mid-1953. But that road to a cessation of hostilities would be punctuated with bitter clashes never to be forgotten by the American military establishment: 'Heartbreak Ridge', 'Old Baldy', 'Hook', 'Triangle Hill', 'White Horse', 'Pork Chop Hill'.

A 10-mile-wide no-man's land now existed between the two protagonists, and in the relative respite, General Van Fleet met with his three corps commanders on 30 April to assess defences along the whole front. Emulating General Ridgway's strategy of employing maximum firepower to save his own manpower, Van Fleet told his senior commanders: 'We must expend steel and fire, not men . . . I want so many artillery holes that a man can step from one to the other.'*

New minefields would be laid, in which would be placed 45-gallon drums of napalm and petrol for electrical detonation. Artillery would be meticulously registered and interlocking groups of machine-gun fire calculated for every single unit. The speed and efficacy of reserve deployments would be optimized, while along the front line a regime of constant probing attacks would be implemented to monitor enemy movements and intentions.

On 7 May, by which time UN forces had retaken Ŭijŏngbu and Ch'unch'ŏn and the ROKA I Corps had almost reached Kansŏng on the east coast, Van Fleet tabled a plan for a full-scale effort to restore Line Kansas, using Line Topeka as a phase line. In the US X Corps sector, Major General Edward M. Almond had positioned the US 1st Marine and US 2nd divisions to cover the Ch'unch'ŏn–Hongch'ŏn axis to the west, leaving the six South Korean divisions from the ROKA III and I corps holding the line in the east of the sector.

---

* David Rees, *Korea: The Limited War* (Pelican Books, Baltimore, 1970).

However, a week later, intelligence of a very large enemy build-up facing the eastern US IX Corps and the US X Corps fronts caused Van Fleet to put his plan on hold. Five Chinese corps—the XII, XV, XX, XXVII and LX—from the CPVA Third and Nineteenth armies were concentrating west of the Pukhan River. Farther east, facing the South Koreans were the KPA V, II and III corps. The enemy was positioning itself, regardless of substantial losses, for Peng Dehuai's second impulse of the spring offensive.

During the night of 15/16 May, an estimated 125,000 Chinese and North Korean troops attacked along a 20-mile front, striking south down the roads from Inje and Ch'unch'ŏn along the Soyang River. Crossing the river to the west of Kwandae-ri, the 81st Division, CPVA XXVII Corps, attacked along the boundary between the ROKA 5th and 7th divisions. Yet again, the South Koreans crumbled, exposing the US II Corps' right flank. By noon the following day—17 May—elements of the ROKA 5th had been reordered south-east of the US II Corps, but of the ROKA 7th, only two battalions of the reserve 3rd Regiment could be located, six miles to the rear near the village of Sangam-ni where they were engaged with the CPVA 81st. To the east, General Almond pulled the ROKA III and I corps back to No Name Line where they held up well to attacks from the 6th and 12th divisions, KPA V Corps, and the 2nd and 27th divisions of the KPA II Corps.

Elements of the US 3rd Ranger Company on patrol, 1951. (Photo US Army)

Government Order No. 13, 1 February 1952

MEDAL OF HONOR
Junior Dean Edwards, Sergeant First Class, Company E, 23rd Infantry Regiment, 2nd Infantry Division, U.S. Army.
Place and date: Near Changbong-ni, Korea, January 2, 1951 [KIA]

Sfc. Edwards, Company E, distinguished himself by conspicuous gallantry and intrepidity above and beyond the call of duty in action against the enemy. When his platoon, while assisting in the defense of a strategic hill, was forced out of its position and came under vicious raking fire from an enemy machine gun set up on adjacent high ground, Sfc. Edwards individually charged the hostile emplacement, throwing grenades as he advanced. The enemy withdrew but returned to deliver devastating fire when he had expended his ammunition. Securing a fresh supply of grenades, he again charged the emplacement, neutralized the weapon and killed the crew, but was forced back by hostile small-arms fire. When the enemy emplaced another machine gun and resumed fire, Sfc. Edwards again renewed his supply of grenades, rushed a third time through a vicious hail of fire, silenced this second gun and annihilated its crew. In this third daring assault he was mortally wounded but his indomitable courage and successful action enabled his platoon to regain and hold the vital strongpoint. Sfc. Edwards' consummate valor and gallant self-sacrifice reflect the utmost glory upon himself and are in keeping with the esteemed traditions of the infantry and military service.

With his right flank now only nominally protected, US 2nd Division commander, Major General Clark L. Ruffner, was once again faced with envelopment from the east. His left and centre well manned by the 38th, 23rd and 9th regiments, and the French battalion as his only divisional reserve, Ruffner reconstituted the proven armour-infantry Task Force Zebra (TF Zebra) to occupy the line on the right. Commanded by Lieutenant Colonel Elbridge L. Brubaker, the force comprised the US 72nd Tank Battalion (less one company), the US 2/23rd, the ROKA 1st Ranger Company, the provisional South Korean Ivanhoe Security Force, and the 3rd Battalion, ROKA 36th Regiment on attachment from the ROKA 5th Division. TF Zebra centred on Route 24, its tanks positioned behind minefields and wire obstacles.

In spite of generally unfavourable weather conditions, the flexibility of FEAF units provided US X Corps with as much air support as General Almond was capable of employing typically three or four airstrikes an hour. On 17 May, the US 2nd Division HQ reported that airstrikes had killed at least 5,000 troops. The following day, the three fast carriers of Task Force 77 arrived on station for added close air-support missions.

French soldiers of the Battalion de Corée on radio watch in central North Korea. (Photo Archive)

Soon after darkness fell on 17 April, elements of CPVA XII Corps attacked the TF Zebra sector, forcing back the South Korean Rangers, the Ivanhoe Security Force and the 3rd Battalion, ROKA 36th Regiment. On the Chinese left, the CPVA 92nd Regiment pressed south along Route 24 in pursuit of the fleeing South Koreans. A little after midnight, leading elements of the CPVA 92nd came under heavy US 72nd Tank

Battalion fire. As the Chinese cleared the road to the left and right, they set off mines and trip flares. Caught against the wire perimeter, combined fire from the infantry and artillery accounted for most of the assailants. Even though the enemy thrust almost reached Hongch'ŏn, the US 2nd Division, with robust air and artillery support, repaired and held the corps' left flank, allowing Van Fleet to concentrate on Almond's centre and right flank where enemy forces were massing.

Almond was of the opinion that Peng Dehuai planned to employ the CPVA XXVII Corps to turn his right flank largely held by South Korean forces. The Chinese general would then strike down the Ch'unch'ŏn–Hongch'ŏn axis with his Third Army. After expressing his concerns to General Van Fleet, the US Eighth Army commander moved the US IX–X boundary 4 miles to the east. In doing so, the US 7th Division took over part of the US 1st Marine Division sector, allowing the latter to relieve the US 9th and 38th regiments for deployment east. To further bolster Almond's sector, Van Fleet moved in the ROKA 8th Division from anti-guerrilla operations to the south. Elements of the US 3rd Division regimental combat teams had already arrived in the sector. For added support, Van Fleet took a battery of 155-mm guns and a battery of 8-inch howitzers from US IX Corps.

Late on 17 May, Almond ordered a four-fold increase in divisional and corps artillery expenditure, blanketing likely enemy lines of approach within 3,000 yards of his defence line. This amounted to the discharge of 41,350 projectiles on 18 May alone.

The availability of as many day and night bomber sorties as US X Corps could coordinate was without a doubt a key determining factor in the successful defence of this sector. Of particular significance was, for the first time in the war, the ability of the USAF to offer the same level of distinguished close-air support in both day and night sorties, a profound improvement in capabilities that prompted FEAF commander General George E. Stratemeyer to comment, 'Enemy frontline troops have now learned that darkness no longer provides a protective cloak against our pinpoint air attacks on their positions.'[*]

In April, the MPQ-radar bombing guidance system control units directed 450 B-29 Superfortress bomb drops on 425 nominated enemy targets. Each heavy bomber carried forty 500-pound proximity-fused fragmentation bombs that detonated at a fixed height above the ground, saturating an area 150 feet in diameter with 15,000 chunks of shrapnel.

In the initial stages of the enemy's new attack on his front, General Almond employed a large number of MPQ-radar directed bombing missions to good effect, but it was his well-conceived strategy of much-increased night bombing sorties that would have the greatest impact on blunting the enemy attacks. Successive daylight massed artillery saturation fire missions and airstrikes would restrict Peng's commanders to reassemble and reinforce their units under cover of darkness. This would be when Almond intended hitting the enemy hardest.

---

[*] Robert Frank Futrell, *The United States Air Force in Korea, 1950–1953* (Progressive Management, 1983).

A B-29 Superfortress takes off at dusk from Japan on a nocturnal interdiction bombing sortie over North Korea. (Photo Air and Space Museum)

The US X Corps G-2 (intelligence) and G-3 (operations) liaised closely to nominate MPQ targets based on information obtained from artillery air observers, observation posts, pilots and POWs. At 6 p.m. on 19 May, Almond reacted to G-2 reports of an imminent enemy attack by implementing his plans for massive night bombing sorties. After eight B-29s blanketed the target area with eighty tons of proximity-fused 500-pound bombs, the enemy attack failed to materialize.

At 8 p.m. the following night, fifteen B-29s executed a second MPQ drop on CPVA troops concentrating just above the US 2nd Division front. The next night—21 May—thirteen B-29s attacked enemy units assembling in the Han'gye and Ch'unch'ŏn areas, resulting in only two CPVA battalions attacking which were easily beaten off. After 20 May, the Chinese and North Koreans ceased making major night attacks. General Ruffner later described the precision radar-guided bombing on his US 2nd Division front, within 400 yards of the CPVA, as 'utterly amazing', and of which General Stratemeyer referred to as 'an epic in our warfare'.[*]

Had it not been for this powerfully destructive close-air support, the US 2nd Division, comprising the 9th, 23rd and 38th infantry regiments, and which included the attached

---

* Ibid.

French Battalion (CO Lieutenant Colonel Magrin Vernerrey) and the Dutch Battalion (CO Lieutenant Colonel W.D.H. Eekhout), may in all likelihood have been overwhelmed with serious loss of life.

Elements of the CPVA 45th Division had in fact infiltrated the US 38th Regiment line on 17 May, but reduced numbers prevented them from retaining the advantage. To the right, the CPVA 181st Division—attached to the CPVA XII Corps—had pushed the French back, exposing the US 23rd Regiment's left flank to attack and threatening Route 24. Once more the South Koreans lacked the mettle to make a stand, as the ROKA 5th Division gave under pressure and withdrew southward.

At this point, Peng had committed the full CPVA XII Corps along General Ruffner's front: the 31st, 34th and 35th divisions. Particularly hard hit, the US 23rd withdrew on Chaun-ni, the 2nd and 3rd battalions abandoning damaged and trapped wheeled vehicles as they fell back. More than 150 trucks loaded with heavy weapons, ammunition and other essential equipment were left behind, while XC Company, US 72nd Tank Battalion lost five tanks. The US 23rd suffered 72 killed, 158 wounded and 190 missing.

By last light on 19 May, to the east of Route 24 the full CPVA Ninth Army faced the US X Corps sector. To the left, on the border with the US IX Corps, the CPVA 180th Division had pushed the UN forces onto the Hongch'ŏn River. Next to the east, the CPVA 45th, 44th, 181st and 35th divisions had forced the line south of Han'gye, while the CPVA 34th and 31st divisions had advanced south of the Naech'on River to the village of Nurŏn-ni on Line Waco at the right boundary of the US 2nd and ROKA 7th divisions. In the latter sector, the CPVA 80th and 79th divisions, and elements of the CPVA 31st Division had taken Habae-jae south of Line Waco, before penetrating deeper below Line Nevada to Route 20 between Changp'yŏng-ni and Soksa-ri, and from there to Hajinbu-ri. There was, however, a perceptible easing in the Chinese momentum, interpreted by General Almond and his command staff as indicative of the enemy regrouping and movingfresh forces to the front in readiness for a renewed attack.

But the damage inflicted on General Peng's troops, particularly on his XII and XV corps, by non-stop UN saturation bombing and rolling artillery barrages was little short of cataclysmic. After five days, the Chinese had broken off the offensive, and withdrawn across the whole front. On 21 May General Van Fleet ordered the ROKA III Corps to restore the enemy salient created by the CPVA south of Line Nevada as he prepared to hit back with all assets at his disposal.

In the west, General Milburn set off his three US I Corps divisions for Line Topeka, anchored on the extreme left at Munsan-ni on the Han River some 15 miles north of his Seoul defences. The counterattack turned out to be uneventful as the KPA I and CPVA LXIII corps' retreat outpaced that of Milburn's troops. To his right, General Hoge's US IX Corps command staff were more cautious, and despite constant urging from the commander and the rapid withdrawal of the CPVA LXIII and LXIV corps, it would be 23 May before Kap'yŏng was retaken. In the US X Corps sector, General Almond had to

A wounded US Marine being attended to by his comrades after the Americans repelled an 800-strong Chinese attack on the Hook. (Photo NARA)

neutralize enemy resistance in the Soksa-ri/Habae-jae/Hajinbu-ri area before pushing his front north below the fleeing enemy to Line Kansas and Yangyang on the east coast.

With this completion of the initial realignment of his trans-peninsular front, on 23 May Van Fleet was ready to launch a massive all-out ground and air counteroffensive with the objectives of the total severance of the enemy's main supply routes to the north and of his destruction.

From Okinawa in Japan, twenty-two B-29 Superfortresses of the 19th and 307th bombardment groups, together with eleven B-26 Invaders of the 3rd Bombardment Group executed MPQ-radar bombing sorties across the whole front, destroying entire enemy battalions and regiments.

UN infantry/armour task forces jumped off next, while the Joint Operations Center (JOC) coordinated close air support by maintaining 'Mosquito' forward air controllers, flying North American T-6Ds over the advancing forces. Reporting every thirty minutes to the JOC, any observations by these US 6147th Tactical Air Control Group 'Mosquitos' of enemy troops and vehicles in the open were given the highest priority for airstrikes against them, even if this meant diverting aircraft on other missions.

With a full complement of FEAF and Task Force 77 assets in support, US I Corps secured the Munsan-ni–Ŭijŏngbu line, while US IX and X corps closed on Line Kansas on the west–east Hwach'ŏn Reservoir–Yangyang axis. At the start of June, with the exception of Kaesŏng in the extreme west, the US Eighth Army had regained full control of South Korean territory. Having restored the 38th Parallel, for General Van Fleet there remained one task: the neutralization of the Iron Triangle north of the 38th.

A name believed to have its origins in the American press of the time to embellish a Korean War hotspot, the Iron Triangle was a triangular North Korean and Communist Chinese concentration and communications hub, bitterly contested throughout the conflict. P'yŏnggang—not to be confused with the North Korean capital P'yŏngyang—sat at the northern apex of the triangle, with Ch'ŏrwŏn to the south-west and Kŭmhwa to the south-east.

On 3 June, Operation Piledriver was launched. US I Corps was to advance on Ch'ŏrwŏn and Kŭmhwa and breach the southern leg of the Iron Triangle, while in the centre US IX Corps was tasked with securing the area from Hwach'ŏn north to Samyang-ni.

A torpedo attack on the Hwach'on Reservoir by Douglas AD Skyraiders of Attack Squadron 195 (VA-195) from USS *Princeton* (CV-37). (Photo US Navy)

On the right, US X Corps was to seize an area from the eastern reaches of the Hwach'ŏn Reservoir to Kŏjin-ni on the east coast. General Almond's greatest challenge was to clear the 'Punchbowl', an appropriately named valley surrounded by hills, 5 miles north of Line Kansas and 19 miles north of the 38th Parallel. A traditional staging ground for communist forces, the Punchbowl remained hotly contested throughout the war, even to the extent of being used as a bargaining tool at truce talks.

Rather unexpectedly however, and particularly in the US I Corps sector, stiff enemy resistance was encountered as the CPVA doggedly refused to relinquish their possession of the Iron Triangle. The US 1st Cavalry Division ran into three lines of CPVA defences in the Yŏnch'ŏn area, and as the US 3rd Division closed on Ch'ŏrwŏn, the Chinese launched a counterattack that pushed one of the battalions back south of the Hant'an River. The US 25th Division battled against well-entrenched Chinese troops below their objective.

The next day, US X Corps continued with what would become a fierce five-day battle for control of the Punchbowl. With only slight progress, the US 7th Marine Regiment was pulled out of reserve and sent to the front, with the US 1st Marine Regiment on the right and the ROKA marines on their left. In a bold and uncharacteristic night attack, at 2 a.m. on 11 June, the ROKA marines surprised a North Korean position, slaughtering most of the enemy and allowing them to move into the Punchbowl.

From last light on 7 June until the night of 9/10 June, B-26 and B-29 bombers from the US 3rd, 98th, 19th and 307th bombardment groups conducted nightly MPQ-directed attacks on enemy positions in and around the Iron Triangle. This allowed the US 3rd Division, the ROKA 9th Division and the 10th Philippine Battalion to take the high ground overlooking Ch'ŏrwŏn, while to the east, the US 25th Divisions and the Turkish Brigade fought their way to within 3 miles of Kŭmhwa.

On 11 June, UN forces entered the now-abandoned two southern towns of the Iron Triangle. Two days later, an armour/infantry task force from each captured town converged on the triangle apex at P'yŏnggang, to find it also deserted. However, the discovery of significant CPVA strengths on high ground commanding P'yŏnggang persuaded General Milburn to withdraw these forces. US IX Corps experienced a very similar situation as it advanced north-east from Kŭmhwa in the direction of Kŭmsŏng. Finding the route blocked with a strong enemy defensive line, the UN forces returned to Kŭmhwa.

The CPVA regained P'yŏnggang a few days later, but the Iron Triangle effectively became a no-man's land, heavily patrolled and ambushed by both sides. The Punchbowl valley had also acquired no-man's land status. Communist forces held the high ground at the northern lip of the 'bowl', while the UN controlled the opposite, southern lip. Over time UN forces at this position included the US 2nd, 3rd 7th and 40th divisions, the US 1st Marine Division and various ROKA divisions, but neither side would attempt to seize the valley itself. Operation Piledriver was the last offensive of the Korean War before the lines above the 38th Parallel settled into a state of stalemate.

A YEAR OF AIR SUPPORT

In the year of combat following the Red aggressions on 25 June 1950, the United Nations Command had defeated numerically superior North Korean and Chinese Communist ground armies.

As their contribution to victory, FEAF airmen had flown 223,000 sorties to drop 97,000 tons of bombs and 7,800,000 gallons of napalm, to fire 264,000 rockets and 98,000,000 rounds of ammunition, and to transport 176,000 tons of cargo and 427,000 passengers and air evacuees.

The FEAF combat sorties had inflicted 120,000 casualties upon the enemy's personnel and had destroyed or damaged 391 aircraft, 893 locomotives, 14,200 railroad cars, 439 tunnels, 1,080 rail and road bridges, 24,500 vehicles, 1,695 tanks, 2,700 guns, and 125,000 buildings which sheltered enemy troops or supplies. FEAF strategic bombers had also neutralized the 18 major strategic targets in North Korea.

In the year FEAF had lost 857 officers and airmen—187 killed, 255 wounded, 412 missing, and 3 known to be prisoners of war. Due to enemy action, FEAF had sustained the loss of 246 aircraft, including 188 fighters, 33 bombers, 9 transports, and 17 other planes. Told in terms of statistics, FEAF's combat record was enviable.

Robert Frank Futrell, *The United States Air Force in Korea, 1950–1953*

An M39 Armored Utility Vehicle of the 3rd Battalion, US 1st Marines, en route to pick up casualties during an attack on the hill known as Boulder City. (Photo NARA)

By mid-1951, a year since North Korean leader Kim Il-sung launched a Soviet-sponsored invasion of South Korea, the warring parties from both sides of the 38th political and ideological divide had experienced short-lived victory and costly defeat. The United States had secured a United Nations mandate to go to war on the Korean peninsula in support of the South under the flag of the international body, ensuring legitimacy by attracting allied forces, among others, from Britain and the Commonwealth.

The entry of hundreds of thousands of 'volunteer' Communist Chinese troops in October 1950 had added a totally new dimension onto the battlefield, which witnessed the UN ground forces reeling back under the sheer weight of Chinese troop numbers.

Now, following several months of seesawing of fortunes which ended in the final Chinese offensive of the conflict, the front was reminiscent of the First World War as the opposing armies faced each other from solidly entrenched defensive lines. The war had entered a stagnant territorial phase, characterized by the heavy employment of artillery and in which limited objectives came at great cost of human life and military ordnance.

Far away from the blood-drenched 38th Parallel, the Soviet chief delegate to the UN, Jacob Malik, and US diplomat George F. Kennan had been meeting in secret to reach a consensus about the need for a ceasefire in Korea. An ardent advocate of the need for containment of Soviet expansionism, Kennan had also been an outspoken critic of General MacArthur's handling of the war. He would be appointed US ambassador to Moscow in December 1951.

On 23 June, in a public broadcast Malik, after accusing the United States and Britain of being 'international warmongers', revealed the outcome of his clandestine meetings with Kennan:

> The Soviet people believe that the most acute problem of the present day—the problem of the armed conflict in Korea—can be settled. They believe that as a first step, discussions should be started between the belligerents for a cease fire and an armistice, providing for the mutual withdrawal of forces from the 38th Parallel.
>
> Can such a step be taken? I think it can, provided there is a sincere desire to put an end to the bloody fighting in Korea. I think that, surely, is not too great a price to pay in order to achieve peace in Korea.*

The willingness of the weary belligerents to enter into truce talks was immediately evident. General Ridgway, in his capacity as commander-in-chief of UN forces, proposed a Danish hospital ship harboured at Wŏnsan as the venue for the commencement of the peace process. However, in a deadly game of chess that would be played out by both sides until the armistice of 27 July 1953 in which north and south strived to seize the initiative in some of the bloodiest fighting of the war, Kim Il-sung and Peng Dehuai insisted on the town of Kaesŏng, the old Korean capital in western Korea.

---

* *Derry Journal*, 25 June 1951.

Although unoccupied at the time, when the talks began on 10 July, Communist forces had moved in. So even before an agenda was drawn up, arguments ensued until 15 July when it was mutually agreed to a Kaesŏng Neutral Zone to which both sides would have equal access. In pursuance of an acceptable agenda, the negotiators, led by KPA Chief of Staff Lieutenant General Nam Il for the North and Vice Admiral C. Turner Joy the South, sat down at the table for the first time. After two weeks of deliberation, an agenda was agreed upon which would direct the delegates to a four-point armistice format:

- Article I: fix a military demarcation line (MDL) and establish a demilitarized zone (DMZ).
- Article II: firm and binding arrangements for a ceasefire, an armistice and the appointment of a supervising organization to oversee the process.
- Article III: arrangements for the repatriation of POWs.
- Article IV: recommendations to the governments of the participating countries.

North Korean General Nam Il arriving at the truce talks at Kaesŏng, September 1952.

On 23 August, the CPVA/KPA delegation unilaterally suspended the talks, ostensibly on the basis that the Americans had conducted bombing raids near Kaesŏng. General Ridgway came out in strong protest, letting it be known that this was a ploy by the communists to buy time in which to regain its military strength in the wake of major losses suffered during the spring offensive. Ridgway was also adamant that he would not return to Kaesŏng unless ordered to do so by Washington. At this point, JCS chairman General Omar N. Bradley and Department of State counsellor Charles E. Bohlen arrived on a fact-finding mission to resolve address Ridgway's concerns. The visitors concurred with the UN commander's contention that the communist delaying tactics at the truce talks at a time when they were militarily weaker, placed the United States at a disadvantage. They also agreed that the communist-chosen venue was wholly unsuitable.

As a consequence, and no doubt with Soviet behind-the-scenes pressure, the truce talks venue was moved a short distance east to P'anmunjŏm, where negotiations resumed on 25 October 1951 and where they would remain until the signing of the armistice.

The Gharry used to transfer pilots to their aircraft at Suwŏn airbase. (Robin Anderson)

6. AT WHAT COST?

'When the enemy's envoys speak in humble terms, but continues his preparations, he will advance. When their language is deceptive but the enemy pretentiously advances, he will retreat. When the envoys speak in apologetic terms, he wishes a respite. When without a previous understanding the enemy asks for a truce, he is plotting. When the enemy sees an advantage but does not advance to seize it, he is fatigued.'

Chinese general, military strategist, writer and philosopher Sun Tzu (544–496 BC)

Casualty statistics attest to the virtually worthless and extremely costly war prosecuted by the UN forces from the commencement of truce talks in July 1951, in a narrow-visioned quest to maintain an upper hand at the negotiating table. In this period, UN forces suffered 60,000 casualties—including 22,000 American—and the Communist forces 234,000. Many of these casualties were sustained in the bloody months of September and October 1951.

From 17 September to 3 October, UN forces conducted operations in the Iron Triangle, codenamed operations Cleanup I and II. As part of General Ridgway's strategy of 'limited objectives', the tactical imperative was to secure a complex of five hills to the west of Ch'ŏrwŏn with the objective of securing the rail route essential for the flow of supplies to the centre of the front. The task, given to the US 3rd Division, would be to seize control of an area known as Bloody Angle, comprising hills 487, 292 and 477.

The next day, in spite of artillery support from the US 9th and 10th FABs and the US 64th Heavy Tank Battalion, the US 7th and 15th regiments failed to take the heavily defended Hill 487. Following nine days of artillery softening during which more than 45,000 artillery, tank and mortar rounds were expended, Cleanup II was launched against the whole hill complex on 29 September. A seven-day battle ensued as A and B companies of the 1st Battalion and E Company of the 2nd Battalion, US 15th Regiment, eventually resulting in the 2nd Battalion taking Hill 487 and the US 65th Regiment the two unnamed two hills in the complex known as Twin Peaks.

From 13 September to 15 October, one of the fiercest and most worthless and wasteful land battles of the Korean War raged. Following earlier inconclusive fighting over possession of the Punchbowl to the north of Inje and above Line Kansas in the US X Corps sector, in three weeks of bitter fighting the US 2nd Division and the ROKA 36th Regiment eventually took Bloody Ridge, a few miles west of the Punchbowl, from KPA forces. But the UN attack came at a cost of 2,700 casualties, mainly from the three US 2nd Division regiments.

Five miles directly to the north, the withdrawing KPA III Corps, commanded by Pang Ho San, had established strong defences on hills 894, 931 and 851, the three peaks that made up a 7-mile-long hill mass that would be dubbed Heartbreak Ridge by American journalists.

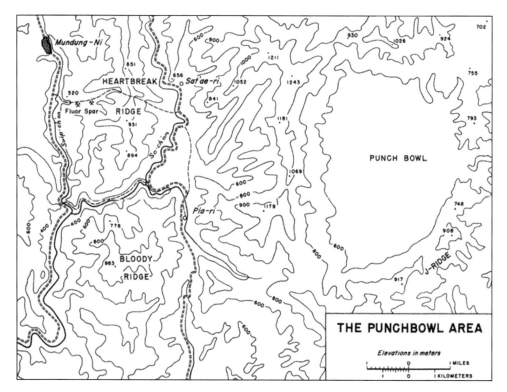

A topographical map showing the heavily contested features known as Punchbowl, Heartbreak Ridge and Bloody Ridge, where successive battles in August and September 1951 resulted in major casualties on both sides. (Map US Army)

Earlier, General Van Fleet had submitted to Tokyo the framework of a plan—called Talons—to straighten out Line Kansas east of Route 29 in the US Eighth Army's eastern front. However, as a clear picture emerged of the heavy toll on Bloody Ridge, Van Fleet elected instead to adhere to the prevailing strategy of patrol, reconnaissance and opportunistic exploitation of limited objectives. Believing that the North Koreans had not recovered from their own substantial losses at Bloody Ridge, Van Fleet sought to hit the KPA on the ridges above before they could recover. General Almond assigned the task to the US 2nd Division, under acting commander Brigadier General Thomas W. de Shazo, who decided to employ his US 23rd Regiment, commanded by Colonel James Y. Adams, and the attached French Battalion, under Lieutenant Colonel Ralph Monclar, for the initial attack.

Colonel Adams would approach the hill complex from the east, moving across the Sat'ae-ri Valley to cut between hills 931 and 851. At this point, one battalion would attack north to take Hill 851, while another struck south to seize hills 931 and 894. On the successful attainment of these objectives, Colonel John M. Lynch's US 9th Regiment would advance to take Hill 728 to the west.

At 5.30 a.m. on the morning of 13 September, 105-mm and 155-mm howitzers, and 8-inch guns from batteries of five field artillery battalions commenced a forty-five-minute barrage of the North Korean positions. Receiving the signal to jump off from regimental HQ, the 3rd Battalion (US 3/23rd), under Lieutenant Colonel Virgil E. Craven, led the advance in a column of companies, followed by the 2nd Battalion (US 2/23rd), commanded by Lieutenant Colonel Henry F. Daniels, as the assault troops moved north from Hill 702 up the Sat'ae-ri Valley.

However, well short of the east–west spur that was to be the access point to Heartbreak Ridge, heavy enemy artillery and mortar fire from the KPA defences on the ridge and from the high ground above the town of Sat'ae-ri pounded the advancing American infantrymen. Heavy casualties notwithstanding, the two battalions inched forward until the US 3/23rd walked into a curtain of machine-gun and rifle fire directed at them from concealed KPA 6th Division bunkers on both sides of the spur. With overtones of Bloody Ridge, the attack ended abruptly, forcing the Americans to dig in for the night in an extremely precarious position at the foot of the spur.

The apocalyptic scene on the fiercely defended Heartbreak Ridge. (Photo NARA)

The next day, General de Shazo redirected Colonel Lynch's US 9th Regiment to attack Hill 894 instead, so as to ease the pressure on the US 23rd. On 15 September, the 2nd Battalion, US 9th Regiment (US 2/9th), with support from B Company, US 72nd Tank Battalion, a company of heavy mortars and a battalion of 155-mm howitzers, moved on the crest of Hill 894 encountering only light resistance. Securing the peak with only 11 casualties, the US 2/9th then faced two days of fierce fighting to hold the hill against concerted KPA counterattacks, in which the Americans suffered a further 200 casualties while remaining unable to assist the US 23rd.

Despite a change of tactics on 16 September from column formation to attacking abreast, and the 1st Battalion (US 1/23rd), under Major George H. Williams, moving on Hill 931 from the south, the US 2/23rd and 3/23rd made slow progress under unrelenting enemy fire. Maintaining control of the gradual access route to Heartbreak Ridge along the Mundung-ni Valley, KPA 6th Division commander General Hong Nim was able to move in the fresh 13th Regiment to relieve the 1st Regiment.

South-west of Heartbreak Ridge, the narrow Pia-ri Valley became a bottleneck of vehicles and civilian porters trying to reach the beleaguered US 23rd with ammunition, food and water. The resultant quagmire presented an easy target for the North Koreans.

On 20 September, Major General Robert N. Young took over command of the US 2nd Division, immediately endorsing Colonel Lynch's plan to widen the attack on Heartbreak Ridge by bringing in the US 1/9th along the Mundung-ni Valley to seize hills 867 and 1024. At the same time, Major General Clovis E. Byers, commander of the US X Corps since mid-July, ordered the ROKA 7th Division to take Hill 1142 about 2,000 yards north-west of Hill 1024.

Against strong resistance, it would be 25 September before the US 1/9th could displace the North Koreans from Hill 1024. As the ROKA 7th Division took Hill 1141 the following day, General Hong moved his KPA 3rd Regiment over from Heartbreak Ridge to counter the new threat from the UN forces. But this reduction in enemy strengths offered the US 23rd no respite.

Having already suffered 950 casualties to his own US 23rd, Colonel Adams informed General Young that the fruitless suicidal attacks were no longer sustainable. With total US 2nd Division casualties now at 1,670, Young called off the operation on 27 September.

After a major revision of tactics and repositioning of infantry and armour, on 4 October the US 2nd Division resumed the attack on Heartbreak Ridge under the codename Touchdown, as forty-nine USMC F-4U Corsairs bombed, rocketed and strafed the North Korean lines.

In a highly coordinated and concentrated series of attacks, before which units of the US 2nd Division even had the luxury of dry-run rehearsals, by 11 October battalions of the US 9th had seized hills 867, 960, 1005 and 666. To the west of the American regiment, the ROKA 8th Division won Hill 1050 and the Kim Il-sung range. The US 1/38th progress was equally successful, jumping off from the abandoned Hill 485 to take Hill 728 a mile to the south, while the US 2/38th struck up the Mundung-ni Valley to seize Hill 636. With these two battalions providing high-ground cover, engineers completed a track to accommodate the advance of Lieutenant Colonel John O. Woods's attached US72nd Tank Battalion.

Waiting for the enemy. US infantrymen on alert in a below-ground-level bunker. (Photo US Army)

Below Heartbreak Ridge, the three US 23rd battalions attacked under US 37th FAB artillery fire, gaining satisfactory ground for the first time in several weeks. Employing small arms, grenades and flamethrowers, the Americans finally neutralized the KPA bunkers that had blocked their way since 13 September. With the French Battalion closing from the north, the US 2/23rd and 3/23rd attacked along the southern approaches of Hill 931 to meet on the summit. After repelling KPA counterattacks, the US 3/23rd moved on to junction with the US 1/23rd for a combined attack on Hill 851, the final Heartbreak Ridge objective.

On the eastern approaches to Hill 851, tanks of the US 23rd's Task Force Sturman had penetrated the Sat'ae-ri Valley to pound KPA defences. To the west, Shermans of the US 72nd Tank Battalion, accompanied by L Company, US 38th, and a platoon of engineers advanced down the newly completed road through the Mundung-ni Valley. Not believing that tanks could possibly use this approach, elements of the KPA V Corps and the CPVA 204th Division were caught in the open busy relieving and replacing units devastated by weeks of UN airstrikes and artillery fire. The tanks, while losing some in the advance, inflicted heavy losses on the Communist forces as the Americans pushed beyond the village of Mundung-ni. In quick succession, the US 38th exploited the arrival of the tanks to take a series of hill objectives before achieving Hill 1220, the regiment's final objective, on 15 October.

Meanwhile on Heartbreak Ridge, the KPA 13th Division defending Hill 851 refused to lay down their arms, electing instead to fight to the last man. With the North Korean division's 21st Regiment to the rear and the 19th Regiment covering the Sat'ae-ri Valley, the sister regiment, the 23rd, defended the peak bunker by costly bunker. Finally, at first light on 13 October, after thirty days of hard fighting, French troops rushed and claimed Hill 851 on behalf of the US 23rd Regiment. However, for the prize of a few miles of real estate, the cost was wholly disproportionate.

The conquest of Heartbreak Ridge had cost the US 2nd Division more than 3,700 casualties, almost half of which were suffered by the US 23rd Regiment and the French Battalion. The division estimated enemy casualties at 25,000. Over the duration of the battle, US M4A3E8 tanks fired 62,000 76-mm rounds, while support artillery contributed 401,000 105-mm howitzer, 84,000 155-mm howitzer and 18,000 8-inch gun rounds. The division's 60-mm, 81-mm and 4.2-inch mortars expended 119,000 bombs. The US Fifth Air Force conducted 842 sorties, dropping 250 tons of bombs on the ridge.

In the interim, Operation Commando had as its objective securing hill positions near Yŏnch'ŏn on the US Eighth Army's left flank. This would advance the UN defences in this sector 6 miles from Line Wyoming to Line Jamestown, thus protecting an extension of the Kŭmhwa–Ch'ŏrwŏn rail line to Seoul. Major General John W. O'Daniel, commander

American M114 155-mm howitzers engaged in some of the heaviest artillery duals at a time when the war had descended into one of maximum firepower for minimal gain. (Photo NARA)

of US I Corps since 19 July, committed five divisions to the operation, while facing him below Line Jamestown were the CPVA XLIV, XLVII, LXIV and LXV corps. The UN forces jumped off at first light on 3 October.

On US I Corps' left flank the ROKA 1st Division, commanded by Brigadier General Bak Lim Hang, was to cross the Imjin River and move on Kaesŏng. The 1st British Commonwealth Division, under General James Cassels, was on the South Koreans' right, tasked with taking the high ground between Samich'ŏn and Kyeho-dong. In the centre the US 1st Cavalry Division, commanded by Major General Thomas L. Harrold, would strike north-west across an 8-mile front between Kyeho-dong and Kamgol. On the corps' right flank, Major General Robert H. Soule's US 3rd Division would advance and seize Hill 281, 6 miles north-west of Ch'ŏrwŏn, and hills 373 and 324, 7 miles west of the town. Soule would also link up with the US 25th Division (US IX Corps) at Chungasan, now under Major General Ira P. Swift, who was advancing on the confluence of the Hant'an and Namdae rivers north-east of Ch'ŏrwŏn. General Harrold had the US 70th Tank Battalion and the US 16th Reconnaissance Company, under Major Carroll McFalls and operating as Task Force Mac, on his left flank.

The divisions on either side of the US 1st Cavalry Division reached Line Jamestown with only light casualties, but it would take General Harrold's men sixteen days of fierce combat and 380,850 rounds from divisional artillery to attain the same objective. Facing Harrold were the well-entrenched and heavily fortified defensive positions of the 139th and 141st divisions, CPVA XLVII Corps, to be joined the next day by the 140th Division.

On day one, the cavalry's advance was slow and costly, with only the US 5th Cavalry taking and holding one intermediate objective: Hill 222. Elements of the US 7th Cavalry had seized but lost hills 418 and 313 to CPVA counterattacks, suffering heavy casualties.

The following day—4 October—elements of the US 8th Cavalry reinforced the US 7th Cavalry for renewed attacks on Hill 418. After hours of brutal, often close-quarter combat, the Americans finally gained the ridges on the western slopes of the hill, only to have the Chinese throw wave upon wave of expendable manpower at them to retake the lost ground. Each CPVA company was equipped with at least ten machine guns, which, with large quantities of hand grenades, caused the bulk of the US 1st Cavalry Division's casualties.

Over the next three days, the American cavalry regiments gradually managed to take and hold high-ground objectives, culminating in the taking of Hill 347 on Line Jamestown by the US 7th Cavalry on 7 October.

However, intensive artillery, tank and mortar fire on the formidable bunker-system stronghold of the CPVA on the high ground above the US 5th Cavalry failed to budge the Chinese. Airstrikes employing napalm and 1,000-pound bombs appeared equally ineffective, as the US 1st Cavalry Division took such a heavy toll, that when an objective was attained its strength was inadequate to repel enemy counterattacks.

Finally, on 13 October the US 8th Cavalry claimed the now-abandoned Hill 272, the eastern approach to the CPVA's last defense line in the sector. Commando was followed by Operation Polecharge, with the objective of clearing a few hills south of Line Jamestown of CPVA positions that remained a threat to the supply routes to Seoul. Lasting from

15–19 October and joined by the Belgian Battalion, the US 5th and 8th Cavalry fought hard to wrest hills 346, 272 and 230 from the Chinese.

Deemed successful, Commando and Polecharge marked the end of strategic territorial operations by UN forces, and as truce talks resumed at P'anmunjŏm, the front remained static. General O'Daniel ordered his corps to dig in and hold the modified line.

However, questions were now being raised in Korea and by the American public if such small gains warranted such a disproportionate loss of troops. US I Corps had sustained 4,000 casualties in the operations, including 2,900 from the US 1st Cavalry Division. In December, the division was relieved by the US 45th Division and withdrawn to Japan, their sixteen-month tour of duty over.

Also, in October, Communist air power noticeably came of age. FEAF discovered that the North Korean airfields at Saamch'ŏn, T'aech'ŏn and Namsi were being repaired and refurbished, and 7,000-foot hard-surfaced runways constructed to accommodate MiG fighter jets. Brigadier General Joe W. Kelly, commander of Bomber Command, tasked with eradicating this threat, planned to deploy flights of three B-29s using short-range navigation guidance beacons (SHORAN) and escorted by F-84 Thunderjets and F-86 Sabres. The latter would engage enemy MiGs to draw them away from the heavy bombers. Conducted in daylight hours, the operations included some of the biggest air battles of the war.

Carrier-borne AD Skyraiders in close air support bomb enemy positions in North Korea. (Photo US Navy)

On 18 October, nine B-29s from the US 19th Bombardment Group (US 19 BG) and another nine from the US 98th Bombardment Wing (US 98 BW) executed unopposed raids on the Saamch'ŏn and T'aech'ŏn airfields, repeating the sorties three days later.

Four days later, nine B-29s, escorted by twenty-four Thunderjets, came under attack from forty MiG-15s while bombing T'aech'ŏn. A B-29 crashed into the sea, but the crew survived. The following day nine B-29s from the US 307th Bombardment Wing (US 307 BW) escorted by twenty-four Thunderjets and with a screening force of thirty-four Sabres, attacked the Namsi airfield. Fifty MiGs arrived, diving through the bomber/escort formations, while another 100 MiGs engaged the Sabres. In the twenty-minute air battle that ensued, each of the three B-29 flights lost an aircraft. Four MiGs were shot down, three by the B-29 gunners, to the loss of one Thunderjet. Only one of the B-29s escaped major damage and without dead and wounded on board.

Notwithstanding the fact that this was described at the time by a USAF officer as 'one of the most savage and bloody air battles of the Korean War', the campaign continued the next day in the same format as before. Targeting railway bridges at Sunch'ŏn, eight B-29s, with sixteen Royal Australian Air Force (RAAF) Gloster Meteor F.8 jet fighters and ten Thunderjets came under attack from seventy MiGs. One B-29 went down and seven sustained major damage.

After a suspension of operations for two days, imposed by FEAF commander General Otto P. Weyland, on 27 October at Sinanju ninety-five MiGs mauled a UN bombing raid which comprised eight B-29s from US 19 BG, sixteen RAAF Meteors and thirty-two Thunderjets. Four B-29s sustained damage, one severely so. The next day, B-29s bombed bridges at Sŏngch'ŏn which, although unchallenged by MiGs, was to be the last daytime bombing mission of this sort.

North American F-86 Sabres of No. 2 Squadron, South African Air Force (front and rear), in formation with No. 77 Squadron, Royal Australian Air Force Gloster Meteors, over the central mountainous plateau of Korea. (Photo Paul du Bois)

In one week, FEAF lost fifteen aircraft, including five B-29s, seven Sabres, two Thunderjets and an RF-80 Shooting Star. Fifty-five crewmen were killed and twelve wounded. Thirty-two MiGs were shot down, of which twenty-four were by Sabres. For the remainder of the war, the communists made little effort to bring the airfields back into operation, switching to airfields in Manchuria safe from UN air attack.

POW: THE FIGHT CONTINUES AFTER THE BATTLE

The Report of the Secretary of Defense's Advisory Committee on Prisoners of War
August 1955

Ordeal by Indoctrination
When plunged into a Communist indoctrination mill, the average American POW was under a serious handicap. Enemy political officers forced him to read Marxian literature. He was compelled to participate in debates. He had to tell what he knew about American politics and American history. And many times the Chinese or Korean instructors knew more about these subjects than he did. This brainstorming caught many American prisoners off guard. To most of them it came as a complete surprise and they were unprepared. Lectures—study groups—discussion groups—a blizzard of propaganda and hurricanes of violent oratory were all a part of the enemy technique.

A large number of American POWs did not know what the Communist program was all about. Some were confused by it. Self-seekers accepted it as an easy out. A few may have believed the business. They signed peace petitions and peddled Communist literature. It was not an inspiring spectacle. It set loyal groups against cooperative groups and broke up camp organization and discipline. It made fools of some men and tools of others. And it provided the enemy with stooges for propaganda shows.

Ignorance lay behind much of this trouble. A great many servicemen were 'teenagers'. At home they had thought of politics as dry editorials or uninteresting speeches, dull as ditchwater. They were unprepared to give the commissars an argument.

Some of the POWs, among them men who became defectors, had heard of Communism only as a name. Many had never before heard of Karl Marx. And here was Communism held up as the salvation of the world and Marx as mankind's benefactor.

The Committee heard evidence which revealed that many of the POWs knew too little about the United States and its ideals and traditions. So the Chinese indoctrinators had the advantage.

On 25 October, truce talks resumed at the new venue of P'anmunjŏm, where they would remain until the July 1953 armistice. During this period, the delegates agreed to armistice supervision by what would be called the Neutral Nations Supervisory Commission (NNSC), made up of representatives from Czechoslovakia, Poland, Sweden and Switzerland. However, negotiations over the repatriation of POWs failed to reach agreement as the communists refused to accept that 60 per cent of their troops held prisoner by the UN did not wish to be repatriated. Away from the negotiating table, political and military manoeuvring became the order of the day as opposing sides strove to attain and retain bargaining superiority. Standing alone, South Korean President Syngman Rhee opposed an armistice from the beginning.

As 1951 drew to a close, the South Koreans launched Operation Ratkiller, a campaign against North Korean troops stranded over time below the 38th Parallel who had resorted to guerrilla warfare and banditry. Under the auspices of the UN Command, the ROKA Capital and 8th divisions were amalgamated into Task Force Paek, named after the South Korean unit commander Lieutenant General Paek Sŏn-yŏp. At the close of the third phase of Ratkiller at the end of January 1952, more than 19,000 guerrillas and bandits had been killed and captured.

On 25 February, the US Fifth Air Force restarted the aerial interdiction of enemy 'choke points' on their main routes of supply in North Korea. In an extremely costly campaign, codenamed Operation Saturate, that was ended in May 1952 with only limited success, the decision had been made to employ fighter-bombers—mainly the North American F-51 Mustang—instead of medium bombers, as the targets would be specific 2-mile-long

Chinese soldiers march American POWs northward into captivity. (Photo Xinhua)

stretches of the railway network in North Korea. By April, the communists had anti-air-craft units at most of these key points, resulting in a significant rise in USAF aircraft losses: 243 fighter-bombers lost and 290 badly damaged. Among the worst hit were the 49th and 136th fighter-bomber wings, whose establishment strengths of 75 aircraft had been reduced to 41 and 39 respectively. Unfortunately, this type of aerial interdiction strategy would be repeated a decade later in Vietnam during Commando Hunt opera-tions, with similar costly and tragic results.

Arguably, one of the biggest farces of the war also occurred in February 1952 with the short-lived initiation of Operation Clam-up. On 10 February, the UN forces ceased all offensive activities along the whole trans-peninsular front: no probing patrols, no provocation, no shooting, no artillery and no air traffic within 12 miles of the front. It was naively thought that this total cessation of all UN hostilities would draw communist forces into the open to investigate what they perceived to have been a withdrawal of UN forces. Large numbers would be killed and captured, bringing the stalemate to an end. The enemy, however, did not fall for the ruse, instead seizing the windfall opportunity of the five-day lull to strengthen their defences.

The nine-month fluctuating fortunes experienced by UN forces fighting over a chunk of high ground above the 45th Division, US I Corps, was typical of this static phase of the conflict. Out of ongoing concern that his US 45th Division troop movements were in full view of the CPVA facing his front, in early June 1952 commander Major General David L. Ruffner set up a network of forward outposts to shield his division. This was achieved with little resistance, with nine outposts successfully established straddling the Yŏkgok-ch'ŏn River valley to the west of Ch'ŏrwŏn at the lower left Iron Triangle. Tactical high points in the hill complex attracted names reflecting the imaginative profiles of the features: White Horse Hill, Arrowhead T-Bone, Alligator Jaws, Arsenal and Eerie. But the heavily defended treeless Hill 275, known as Old Baldy, and its northern neighbour Hill 234, or Pork Chop Hill, at first remained in Chinese hands.

White Horse Hill, situated to the north of the Yŏkgok-ch'ŏn River, was deemed to be of strategic importance to US IX Corps in that its possession protected the Ch'ŏrwŏn supply route. For similar reasons, on 6 October 1952, the CPVA launched its biggest offensive of the year, as two battalions of the 340th Regiment, 114th Division, CPVA XXXVIII Corps, attacked the hill. Defending the feature was the ROKA 9th Division, commanded by Major General Kim Jong-oh, but this was no longer the weak-willed South Korean military of earlier months. Trained and equipped to a much higher stand-ard, Kim Jong-oh also enjoyed the added support of artillery, armour, rocket launchers, anti-aircraft weaponry and the US Fifth Air Force.

Over a period of nine days, possession of White Horse Hill changed twenty-four times as 23,000 CPVA troops, from seven of the CPVA XXXVIII's nine regiments, attacked the South Koreans. The USAF flew 669 daytime and 76 night sorties in support, dropping 2,700 general-purpose and 358 napalm bombs, and firing 750 5-inch rockets, while corps artillery expended 185,000 rounds on the CPVA. On 15 October, the Chinese withdrew,

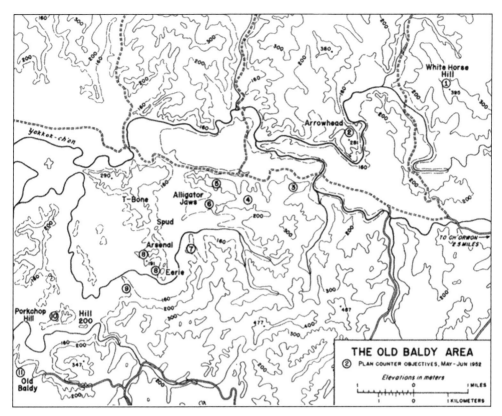

From June 1952 to March 1953, the high ground commanding the supply route through the Yŏkgok-ch'ŏn River valley was the scene of continuous fighting, making the names of Old Baldy and Pork Chop Hill synonymous with the Korean War. (Map US Army)

leaving the hill in South Korean hands, but at great cost to both sides. The ROKA 9th Division suffered 3,500 casualties and the CPVA an estimated 15,000.

As the White Horse Hill battle neared a satisfactory outcome for the defending UN forces, General Van Fleet turned his attention to the so-called Triangle Hill Complex, an area of commanding landscape 3 miles north of Kŭmhwa on the Iron Triangle's eastern point. Centred on Hill 598, known as Triangle Hill, the Chinese position was only 200 yards from the UN front. Predicting potential UN troop losses at 200, on 13 October Van Fleet launched Operation Showdown, with the objective of taking Triangle Hill, thereby forcing the CPVA back to the next hill complex 1,250 yards farther away. It had been planned that the operation would be supported by 288 artillery pieces from 16 battalions and a minimum of 200 fighter-bomber sorties. But after only two days, the air support was diverted to the battle for White Horse Hill.

The task of taking Triangle Hill was assigned to recently appointed Colonel Lloyd R. Moses's US 31st 'Polar Bears' Regiment by US 7th Division commander General Smith.

The two battalions employed by Moses encountered fierce opposition from an elite battalion of the 135th Regiment, 45th Division, CPVA XV Corps, who repulsed the American attack on 14 October. The following day, Moses's troops seized Triangle Hill, at great cost to both sides, with the US 7th Division expending a battalion a day, suffering 2,000 casualties in twelve days of fighting.

On 25 October the American division was relieved by the ROKA 2nd Division, who held Triangle Hill for a further five days before being forced off by the Chinese. On 5 November, Major General Reuben E. Jenkins, commander of the US IX Corps since 9 August, called off the UN attack on the basis of very high casualty numbers. The UN forces had sustained around 9,000 casualties when Jenkins ceded Triangle Hill to the CPVA, who by this time had suffered 19,000 casualties.

A seemingly endless cycle of attack and counterattack saw possession of Old Baldy and Pork Chop Hill seesaw between the two sides several times over the following months, until 23 March 1953 when the CPVA launched a 3,500-strong attack against the outposts. By this time, the 31st Regiment, US 7th Division, commanded by Colonel William B. Kern, was responsible for the defence of the area around Old Baldy. Dug in on the Old Baldy peak and commanded by Lieutenant Colonel Alberto Ruiz-Novoa, was the attached battalion from Colombia, the only South American country to join the UN forces in Korea. On Pork Chop Hill, the 21st Thai Infantry Battalion, attached the US 2nd Division, was ready to defend the hill once more, in a fight for which they would be best known in the war.

An intensive artillery and mortar bombardment preceding the Chinese attack destroyed most of the bunkers. Having seized Old Baldy, the CPVA repulsed a US 31st Regiment counterattack, inflicting heavy casualties. The following night, Colonel Kern withdrew his troops, abandoning any hope of regaining Old Baldy. The remnants of the defeated Colombians escaped during the night. Lieutenant General Maxwell D. Taylor, who had replaced General Van Fleet as US Eighth Army commander on 11 February 1953, now decided that possession of Old Baldy was no longer essential and cancelled all plans for its recapture.

After UN forces retook Pork Chop Hill in a counterattack on 24 March, the hill position, now extending into enemy lines, was maintained as a fortified outpost, ensuring that Pork Chop Hill would be remembered for the costly, bloody and ultimately futile battles for possession.

At 10 p.m. on 16 April, CPVA 201st Regiment troops stealthily arrived at Pork Chop Hill, where they quickly overwhelmed outpost elements of E Company, US 31st Regiment. This was followed by an artillery-supported attack during which company commander First Lieutenant Thomas U. Harrold's hilltop defences were overrun.

Just before dawn—17 April—two US 31st Regiment companies, K, under First Lieutenant Joseph G. Clemons and L, under First Lieutenant Forrest J. Crittendon, launched a counterattack, reaching the main trenches on Pork Chop Hill as it became light. By then the Americans had already sustained 50 per cent losses, with half of L Company trapped in the outpost trenches on Hill 200 to the right. Repeated attacks

Troops of the Korean service corps unload timber from an M39 Armored Utility Vehicle on Old Baldy near Ch'ŏrwŏn, Korea. (Photo NARA)

by the Americans were repelled, during which confusion arose, resulting in incidents of units taking friendly fire.

Responding to Lieutenant Clemons's urgent request for reinforcements, G Company, US 17th Regiment, attached to the US 31st, were rushed forward, where company commander First Lieutenant Walter B. Russell linked up at 8.30 a.m. with Clemons (his brother-in-law) who was in charge of the attack. Artillery fire from both sides now pounded the hilltop, preventing either belligerent from achieving a conclusive result.

Arising out of misunderstood communications between rear echelons, Russell's G Company was withdrawn at 3 p.m. after suffering heavy losses. The status of the two US 31st companies, however, was not sought, and it would only be a while later that news came through that they were down to twenty-five survivors. At this time the US 7th Division commander, Major General Arthur G. Trudeau, arrived at the US 31st HQ where he placed Colonel Kern in command of the operation.

Kern's priority was to relieve the decimated K and L companies, initially sending Captain Monroe D. King's F Company, US 17th Regiment, up the hill under heavy Chinese artillery fire. It took King only thirty minutes to reach the trenches, but in that time nineteen of his men were killed. Just before midnight, E Company, US 17th, under First Lieutenant Gorman C. Smith, jumped off to reinforce F Company. After twenty hours of fierce fighting, only 7 of the original 135 members of K Company walked down the hill—the rest were casualties, including 18 killed. Several of the L Company survivors remained behind to show the relief companies around the defences.

At 1.30 a.m.—18 April—battalion-strength elements of the CPVA 201st Regiment attacked once more, inflicting heavy casualties and almost overrunning F Company. Fortuitously, Lieutenant Smith had led his E Company on a different approach to the hill to avoid enemy artillery, and in doing so surprising the Chinese assailants on their flank and forcing them to break off their attack. Company-strength troops of the CPVA 141st Division were unsuccessful in subsequent attempts to dislodge the Americans at 3.20 a.m. and 4.20 am. At first light, A Company, US 17th Regiment, joined her two sister companies on Pork Chop Hill.

That afternoon, the battle ended, until 9/10 July 1953 when both CPVA divisions massed to launch several attacks on the five battalions of the 17th and 32nd regiments, US 7th Division, defending Pork Chop Hill. On the morning of 11 July, US I Corps commander, Major General Bruce C. Clark, ordered Pork Chop Hill to be abandoned to the Chinese. The signing of the armistice was only a fortnight away.

The successive battles for a hill that would ultimately be gifted to the enemy cost the lives of 243 American troops, of which the bodies of 163 were never recovered. A further 916 were wounded and 9 taken prisoner. Chinese losses were estimated at 1,500 killed and 4,000 wounded.

The last major limited-objective operations of 1952, and which lasted until the armistice, were the four battles over ownership of a hook-shaped hill feature in the US I Corps sector, situated north of the 38th Parallel above Seoul. Dominating the Samich'ŏn Valley. The Hook was situated in the Nevada Complex overlooking the vital north-west approaches to the South Korean capital.

Having transferred earlier in the year from the US X Corps to US I Corps—now commanded by Lieutenant General Paul W. Kendell—the US 1st Marine Division, under the highly decorated Major General Edwin A. Pollock, was positioned on Line Jamestown, south-west of the Samich'ŏn River and on the left flank of the British 1st Commonwealth Division. Facing an estimated 49,800 Chinese troops of the CPVA LXIII and LXV corps, the US 7th Marine Regiment (US 7th Marines), established seven named outposts in the Nevada Complex, before siting Outpost Warsaw on the Hook, at a point where the line jutted out three miles north of the Imjin River. Outpost Verdun was then established on the US 7th Marines border with the British Commonwealth division.

In the first few days of the first battle, the 1st and 3rd battalions, US 7th Marines, lost and retook Outpost Warsaw, but were unable to regain Outpost Seattle. By 6 October, all three Marine battalions had established a defensive line: the 2nd on the left, 3rd in the centre and the 1st on the right. While incurring increased losses, by last light the Marines had been unsuccessful in infiltrating the Chinese defences on Seattle. The following day,

Outpost Frisco was abandoned, adding to the lost Seattle and Detroit. The US 7th Marines had now sustained 10 killed, 22 missing and 125 wounded, 105 so seriously that they required evacuation. A lull in the fighting followed, during which the US 5th Marines relieved the US 1st Marines at the centre of the division's line.

During the hours of darkness on the night of 24/25th, in a fierce exchange of artillery and mortar fire between batteries of both the US 11th Marines and the CPVA batteries, around 7,000 Chinese attacked the Hook, defended by 3,850 Marines, with 'support' from 746 members of the Korean Service Corps, with their 18 interpreters, 133 Marines hospital personnel, 11 US Navy medical officers and 3 signalmen. While the intensive artillery duel showed no signs of letting up, the first land-based Grumman F-9F Panther fighters from Marine Attack Squadron 311 (VMA-311) pounded massing enemy troops with high-explosive and napalm bombs.

Severe artillery and mortar damage to Australian positions on the Hook. (Photo AWM)

Just after 6 p.m. on 26 October, CPVA troops attacked and overran Outpost Ronson, while a sister company executed a two-pronged attack on Warsaw. The Marines fought back with anything and everything as the Chinese swarmed over their position, even using rifles to bludgeon the enemy when ammunition ran out. After four hours of not hearing from Warsaw, Colonel T.C. Moore, commanding the US 7th Marines reluctantly had to assume that Warsaw had fallen and the defenders all killed or captured.

In the early hours of 27 October, General Pollock ordered the 3/1st Marines, under Lieutenant Colonel Sidney J. Altman, from reserve into the US 7th Marines sector, tasked with mounting a counterattack on the Hook. In preparation, concentrated artillery, tank and mortar fire pounded the CPCV position, while Grumman F7F Tigercat heavy night fighters from the US 1st Marine Air Wing bombed immediate enemy supply routes.

By midday the Marines' counterattack was entering its final phase as I, H and B companies advanced on the Hook and Warsaw under heavy CPVA artillery and mortar fire. At 4.35 p.m., despite sustaining significant losses, I Company moved onto the Hook summit where work commenced on clearing badly damaged trenches and bunkers. Around midnight B Company were closing in to the left of I Company, but after engaging the Chinese defenders in a vicious firefight for almost two hours,

Elements of the Black Watch (Royal Highland Regiment) take a break on their way to the Hook. (Photo MoD)

the Marines had to break off to call for artillery and mortar support to soften the enemy positions.

At 3.40 a.m.—28 October—B Company penetrated the CPVA defences and by first light had secured the Hook. Nearby, elements of the US 7th Marines retook Warsaw and Ronson. The repossession of the Hook had cost the Marines 70 killed, 386 wounded, 12 missing and 27 taken prisoner. In November, it would be the turn of the British 1st Commonwealth Division, after relieving the US 1st Marine Division in the sector, to resist powerful efforts by the Chinese to retake the Hook.

In mid-April 1952, the 1st Commonwealth had been deployed in between the US 1st Marine Division, on the left, and the US 45th Division. The 1st Commonwealth now comprised three infantry brigades:

25th Canadian Brigade (25th Canadian) (Brigadier Patrick Bogert)
1st Battalion, the Royal Canadian Regiment (1/RCR) (Lieutenant-Colonel Peter Bingham)
1st Battalion, Princess Patricia's Canadian Light Infantry (1/PPCLI) (Lieutenant-Colonel John Cameron)
1st Battalion, Royal 22nd Regiment (Royal 22nd) (Lieutenant-Colonel Louis Trudeau)

28th Commonwealth Brigade (28th British) (Brigadier Tom Daly)
1st Battalion, the Royal Fusiliers (1/RF) (Lieutenant-Colonel Dick Stevens)
1st Battalion, the Durham Light Infantry (1/DLI) (Lieutenant-Colonel Peter Jeffreys)
1st Battalion, Royal Australian Regiment (1/RAR) (Lieutenant-Colonel Ian Hutchison)
3rd Battalion, Royal Australian Regiment (3/RAR) (Lieutenant-Colonel Ron Hughes)

29th British Infantry Brigade (29th British) (Brigadier A.H.G. Ricketts)
1st Battalion, the King's Regiment (Liverpool) (1/KR) (Lieutenant-Colonel Archie Snodgrass)
1st Battalion, the Duke of Wellington's Regiment (1/DW) (Lieutenant-Colonel F.R. St P. Bunbury)
1st Battalion, the Black Watch (1/BW) (Lieutenant-Colonel David Rose)

After the exhausting fighting just days before, US I Corps commander General Kendell relieved the US 1st Marine Division from the Hook sector to recover. As they withdrew, the 29th British assumed responsibility for the left and the 28th British for the right of the sector, while the 25th Canadian moved into reserve. The ROKA 1st Division took over the extreme right of the line between the Imjin River and Hill 355, known locally as Kowang-san and by UN troops as 'Little Gibraltar'.

When the 1/BW took over the war-devastated Hook summit, the British 55 Field Squadron, Royal Engineers, moved in to construct more robust bunkers, deep communication trenches, tunnels and underground shelter chambers. Work would still be ongoing when the CPVA launched their first attack.

THE LONDON GAZETTE, TUESDAY, 25 DECEMBER 1951

The KING has been graciously pleased to approve the award of the VICTORIA CROSS to:

14471590 Private William Speakman, Black Watch (Royal Highland Regiment), attached to the 1st Battalion The King's Own Scottish Borderers.

From 0400 hrs., 4th November, 1951, the defensive positions held by 1st Battalion The King's Own Scottish Borderers were continuously subjected to heavy and accurate enemy shell and mortar fire. At 1545 hrs., this fire became intense and continued thus for the next two hours, considerably damaging the defences and wounding a number of men.

At 1645 hrs. the enemy in their hundreds advanced in wave upon wave against the King's Own Scottish Borderers' positions, and by 1745 hrs. fierce hand-to-hand fighting was taking place on every position.

Private Speakman, a member of "B" Company, Headquarters, learning that the section holding the left shoulder of the company's position had been seriously depleted by casualties, had had its N.C.Os. wounded and was being over-run, decided on his own initiative to drive the enemy off the position and keep them off it. To effect this, he collected quickly a large pile of grenades and a party of six men. Then, displaying complete disregard for his own personal safety, he led his party in a series of grenade charges against the enemy; and continued doing so as each successive wave of enemy reached the crest of the hill. The force and determination of his charges broke up each successive enemy onslaught and resulted in an ever-mounting pile of enemy dead.

Having led some ten charges, through withering enemy machine-gun and mortar fire, Private Speakman was eventually severely wounded in the leg. Undaunted by his wounds, he continued to lead charge after charge against the enemy, and it was only after a direct order from his superior officer that he agreed to pause for a first field dressing to be applied to his wounds. Having had his wounds bandaged, Private Speakman immediately rejoined his comrades and led them again and again forward in a series of grenade charges, up to the time of the withdrawal of his company at 2100 hrs.

At the critical moment of the withdrawal, amidst an inferno of enemy machine-gun and mortar fire, as well as grenades, Private Speakman led a final charge to clear the crest of the hill and hold it, whilst the remainder of his company withdrew. Encouraging his gallant but by now sadly depleted party, he assailed the enemy with showers of grenades and kept them at bay sufficiently long for his company to effect its withdrawal.

Under the stress and strain of this battle, Private Speakman's outstanding powers of leadership were revealed, and he so dominated the situation that he inspired his comrades to stand firm and fight the enemy to a standstill. His great gallantry and utter contempt for his own personal safety were an inspiration to all his comrades. He was, by his heroic actions, personally responsible for causing enormous losses to the enemy, assisting his company to maintain their position for some four hours and saving the lives of many of his comrades when they were forced to withdraw from their position.

Private Speakman's heroism under intense fire throughout the operation and when painfully wounded was beyond praise and is deserving of supreme recognition.

Private Bill Speakman of the Black Watch (Royal Highland Regiment), attached to the 1st Battalion, King's Own Scottish Borderers during the Korean War, was awarded the Victoria Cross for gallantry in battle in November 1951.

Early evening on 18 November, two CPVA companies overwhelmed a 1/BW outpost and commenced a three-prong attack on the Hook. Observing the battle from 2,500 yards away on Yong-dong, 1/DW opened machine-gun fire on the Chinese attackers across the Samich'ŏn in an enfilade that lasted all of eleven hours. In added support, divisional artillery expended 50,000 rounds on the same target.

Following a lull in the fighting, at around midnight the Chinese attacked again with renewed momentum, this time gaining a foothold on the hilltop. Searchlights revealed the sheer weight of the attack, prompting Colonel Rose to deploy Centurion tanks of B Squadron, the 5th Royal Inniskilling Dragoons, to assist the Black Watch with their hold on the Hook.

By first light, the fighting still raged. One of the Centurions had been knocked out, but the enemy had been prevented from taking the hill. The CPVA broke off their attack and the Scots surfaced from the relative safety of their tunnels and underground chambers, realizing they had held the position. Elements of the Canadian brigade immediately relieved 1/BW to see to their casualties.

At the end of January 1953, the British 1st Division was placed in reserve, before redeployment in April. Together with 1 Troop, British 55 Field Squadron, 1/BW returned to the Hook hill complex, positioning a company on each of the Hook, Sausage, and points 121 and 146. Shelling and mortaring continued as both sides targeted the other's routes of supply. After the Scots and the sappers had done their best to strengthen physical defences in a scene reminiscent of the Western Front, on the night of 12/13 May, 1/DW—the 'Dukes'—relieved the Black Watch. The Scots had lost twelve killed, seventy-three wounded and twenty missing, presumed taken prisoner.

On the night of 28 May, there was a significant increase in CPVA bombardment of the Hook, 11,000 rounds raining down on the Dukes' positions. The inevitable waves of attack followed, during which troops of the CPVA 133rd Division would have overrun the British had it not been for artillery support from the British 25-pounders and US I Corps 155-mm, 24-0mm, 8-inch and rocket fire. Centurion tanks from C Squadron, British 1st Royal Tank Regiment, weighed in with 20-pounder shells from the tanks' 84-mm guns.

Chinese troops reaching the Dukes' defences employed satchel bombs and incendiaries to all but destroy remaining British defences. However, fierce close-quarter combat drove the CPVA off, and as day broke, two troops of the 55 Field Squadron went into the forward company positions to restore a semblance of defence perimeters. Chinese 60-mm mortars hampered the sappers' work, the enemy firing positions so close that the mortar bombs could be heard being discharged from the tubes.

The CPVA finally broke off their attack as the Dukes doggedly clung to their position on the Hook, losing twenty killed, eighty-six wounded and twenty missing. In recognition of their brave stand, the Duke of Wellington's Regiment was awarded the battle honour 'The Hook 1953' and the renaming of the 1st Battalion's HQ Company to Hook Company.

The final battle for control of the Hook took place just days before the signing of the armistice. With the truce talks at P'anmunjŏm nearing conclusion, the Chinese launched

Troops of the 1st Battalion, The Duke of Wellington's Regiment, at a bunker on the Hook. (Photo MOD)

a last-ditch attack on the Hook with the hope of a telling victory before a ceasefire. Between 24–26 July, the CPVA 137th Division would attack 2/RAR's and the US 7th Marines' positions on Line Jamestown.

By mid-July 1953, the 28th British, commanded by Australian, Brigadier John Wilton, had taken over the defence of the Hook on the 1st Commonwealth Division's left. At the time, the brigade comprised the Australian 2/RAR and 3/RAR, and two British battalions, the 1/DLI and the 1/RF. Among the support were the 16th Field Regiment, Royal New Zealand Artillery and C Squadron, the British 1st Royal Tank Regiment. equipped with Centurion tanks. The 25th Canadian Brigade would defend hills 355 and 159 on the right. The ROKA 1st Division held the Commonwealth division's right flank.

The Commonwealth's left flank was held by the US 1st Marine Division, commanded by Major General Randolph Pate. In this sector, the US 7th Marine Regiment under Colonel Glenn C. Funk occupied the Marines' right flank and the US 5th Marine Regiment the centre. The US 1st Marine Regiment held the rear in divisional reserve, while artillery support would be provided by the US Marine 11th Regiment. At this time, the I, XLVI, LXIII, LXIV and LXV corps of the CPVA Nineteenth Army Group, commanded by Huang Yongsheng, faced US I Corps.

A 1st Battalion, King's Regiment M1919 Browning machine-gun post on the Hook. (Photo Sergeant Mark Carson)

Initially, while the CPVA focused on the US 7th Marines to the south-west of 2/RAR, the Australians repaired and strengthened defences. From 21–24 July, in the light of air reconnaissance discovering a build-up of Chinese forces west of the Samich'ŏn River, night patrols were conducted to prevent surprise enemy attacks. Despite strong rumours of a ceasefire, enemy artillery bombardment increased significantly in preparation for an attack on 2/RAR and the US 7th Marines on their left flank.

During the night of 24/25 July, from 9 p.m. the CPVA launched several unsuccessful attacks on the Australians, before turning their attentions on the US 7th Marines on Hill 111, known as Boulder City, and the neighbouring 3rd Battalion, US 1st Marines on Hill 119. A company of 1/DLI was brought up in reserve to the left of 2/RAR, and a reserve 3/RAR company placed on emergency standby. While close-quarter fighting raged on Hill 119, the CPVA 408th Regiment launched an attack against the US 5th Marines in the centre.

By first light, the UN forces were holding their positions, largely thanks to supporting artillery to counter the constant Chinese barrage. The US 11th Marines and the British and New Zealand guns fired 37,000 rounds during the night.

Bombardment of the UN positions and the CPVA assailants continued unabated on 25 July. More determined CPVA attacks across the Nevada Complex continued that night, with the enemy reaching forward Marines trenches before being driven back between 1.30 a.m. and 3 a.m.

For the second night, the Marines and the Australians had withstood great pressure from the Chinese, and again support artillery had played a key role. Of the 9,500 rounds expended by divisional artillery, the New Zealand had fired 5,700 rounds, employing air-burst proximity-fused ordnance to inflict severe casualties on the attacking CPVA. As the enemy withdrew and recovered their wounded, it was estimated that the Chinese had suffered almost 3,000 killed on the approaches to the 2/RAR position, largely due to fire

Wreckage of a Jeep and a 15-cwt truck on the rear slope of the Hook near the Black Watch defensive position. (Photo MoD)

from the 163 Battery, 16th Royal New Zealand Artillery. Battery commander, Major James Spence, who personally directed his guns from a forward position, would be awarded the Military Cross. Lieutenant P.O.G. Forbes of 2/RAR would also receive the Military Cross for his bravery in the defence of their position.

In the two days and nights of fighting, the Australians lost five killed and twenty-four wounded, while 2/RAR over the previous two weeks on the Hook had 17 killed and 31 wounded. Over the same two nights, the Marines had lost 43 killed and 316 wounded, bringing their total casualties for July to 181 killed and 1,430 wounded.

In the three months leading up to the signing of the armistice, both UN and CPVA forces suffered major casualties as both sides fought bitterly, and with no apparent consideration of cost, for little or no tactical advantage. In this period, the UN forces sustained 65,000 casualties and the CPVA more than 135,000—a waste that had no tangible influence on the outcome of the truce talks.

Since the cessation of open hostilities in July 1953, historians and analysts have continued to interpret the veracity and plausibility of military and civilian casualty figures, particularly those of North Korea and Communist China.

Among the United Nations Command armed forces' casualties, the statistics are, understandably, dominated by those of the United States. For purposes of data collation, over the decades there have been varying applications of the definition of casualty classifications such as killed in action (KIA), died of wounds (DOW), wounded in action (WIA), missing in action (MIA), prisoner of war (POW) and unknown. For example, the Department of the Army only considered the death in action of an American serviceman if his body had been recovered. Official South Korean statistics for ROKA casualties, owing to rudimentary medical services, vary a great deal. Civilian casualty figures north and south of the 38th Parallel remain largely speculative as a result of either statistic embellishment for propaganda purposes or simply because counts were simply not possible in many areas of the Korean theatre.

The author has used the comprehensive and authoritative 2002 publication *Encyclopedia of the Korean War: A Political, Social, and Military History*, edited by Spencer C. Tucker (Checkmark Books, New York) as his source for casualty figures:

- US armed forces, 140,200, including 33,667 KIA, DOW, MIA.
- ROKA, an estimated 974,000, including 257,000 KIA, DOW, MIA.
- Communist China admits to 370,000, including 125,400 'combat deaths'. US Army estimates are 1 million including 500,000 KIA.
- North Korea, estimated by South Korea at 295,000 deaths (no figure ever given by P'yŏngyang).
- UN allied forces, 15,488, including 11,528 KIA, DOW, MIA.
- Of the 13 allied forces, included in the figures above, the largest number of casualties sustained was the United Kingdom with 3,754 (2,674 deaths) and Turkey, with 3,000 (889 deaths).

A US Marine Corps chaplain consoles a battle-weary corpsman in Korea. (Photo USMC)

Civilian casualty figures for the true victims of the conflict will forever remain in the realms of speculation. South Korean figures vary considerably between 244,000 and 991,000, including 129,000 massacred by the North Koreans. Also included is an estimated 200,000 abducted and pressganged into KPA service. The United Nations believes that a figure of 900,000 deaths is 'not unreasonable'. Comparative civilian death figures for North Korea have never been officially disclosed, resulting in a vague estimation by historians of up to 2 million.

7. QUO VADIS?

'Past records of inter-Korean relations show that confrontation between fellow country-men leads to nothing but war.'

North Korean leader Kim Jong-un

The signing of the armistice by the United States, China and North Korea, but not South Korea as President Rhee had refused to do so, silenced the guns in a ceasefire. Across the demilitarized zone divide, the two opposing sides on the Korean peninsula remain in a de jure state of war.

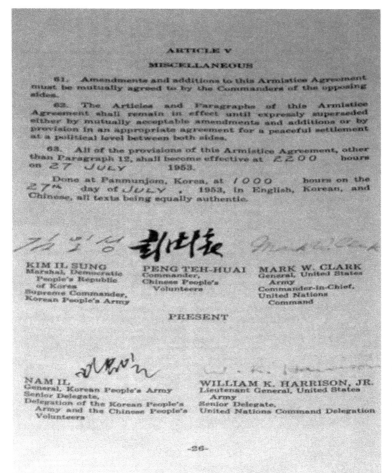

The signatory page of the Korean War Armistice, dated 27 July 1953. South Korean President Syngman Rhee refused to be party to the truce.

Prior to 1905, when Imperial Japanese troops marched into Korea, the territory had been the domain of 500 years of monarchic rule. The tripartite Potsdam Conference of July–August 1945 was the final in a litany of meetings at which the 'Big Powers' decided on the complexion of a post-Second World War world, and where agreement was reached on the immediate future of Korea, which had been annexed and occupied by Japan since 1910. The big-power divide was set at the 38ºN line of latitude, a seemingly arbitrary delineation that would be known as the 38th Parallel. Interim custodianship would be undertaken by the United States and the Soviet Union, pending democratic elections for a unified independent state of Korea.

With the capitulation of Japan on 15 August 1945, bringing the Second World War to an end, Soviet and American troops moved into their respective northern and southern administrative zones to commence the massive exercise of disarming and repatriating 600,000 Japanese military personnel and 70,000 civil servants from Korea.

In May 1948, the North refused to participate in elections for a 200-seat constituent assembly in a unified Korea. However, the United Nations endorsed the legitimacy of the outcome, recognizing South Korean president Syngman Rhee's new government. North Korea distanced itself from the South-only elections, proclaiming in September the communist Democratic People's Republic of Korea, with Kim Il-sung as its leader.

By December, Soviet and US forces, in pursuance of Potsdam, respectively withdrew from north and south of the 38th Parallel. For the United States, South Korea was of no regional importance, and therefore Washington saw no need to equip the South with military hardware with which to defend itself. For the North, Stalin's agenda for the peninsula could not have been more different. Moscow selected, groomed, indoctrinated, and trained and equipped Kim Il-sung and his army. Stalin then sat back, having significantly created a vast swathe of red to the south of his vast nation.

On 25 June, under persuasion from Moscow, North Korea launched a massive attack on the South, crossing the 38th Parallel. In Washington and Tokyo, the Americans were caught totally by surprise, with most enjoying a leisurely weekend away from the office. Ill-prepared and poorly equipped, South Korean and US forces, thrown in to execute holding-only positions, suffered humiliating defeat after defeat as the North Koreans swept down the peninsula, in an invasion reminiscent of Hitler's blitzkrieg across a helpless Western Europe.

Days later, the United Nations Security Council adopted Resolution 84, calling on member states to assist with whatever means at their disposal to clear the South of the North Korean invaders. The controversial Second World War US army veteran and icon, General Douglas MacArthur, was appointed commander of United Nations Command forces, tasked with the implementation of the UN resolution.

At the end of July, the retreating US and South Korea forces were finally able to make a stand in an enclave in the south-eastern tip of the peninsula: the Pusan Perimeter. Here, Lieutenant General Walton Walker, commander of the US Eighth Army, displayed extraordinary leadership by employing mobile-defence tactics to successfully halt the North Korean advance.

In Tokyo, MacArthur sought to exploit Walker's successful stand on the Pusan Perimeter. Against all odds, on 15 September 1950, the US X Corps executed a daring amphibious assault on the west coast Korean port of Inch'ŏn. In the ensuing days following the establishing of four beachheads, MacArthur fulfilled his master plan of enveloping the entire North Korean invasion force, with General Walker breaking out of the Pusan Perimeter from the south.

The North Koreans' initial thrust down the Korean peninsula was almost entirely as a result of the element of surprise, as US intelligence had failed to assess an imminent threat to South Korea, predicting instead that Nationalist Chinese Formosa faced invasion by Mao Zedong's communist forces.

On 1 October, frustrated by a lack of progress in the UN General Assembly to approve a road map for Korea's future, South Korean President Syngman Rhee ordered his troops into North Korea. Just over a week later, General MacArthur ordered US I Corps in the west and US X Corps in the east to force the 38th Parallel. Typically, the UN forces

The flags of the contributing United Nations countries at the Korean War Memorial, Washington State Capitol, Olympia, USA. (Photo Bluedisk)

commander's commitment was absolute, but the high-risk imponderables were also many, not least of all how Moscow and Beijing might react.

However, the egocentric, independently minded MacArthur, flying high from his Inch'ŏn masterstroke and the accompanying adulation from the American public, pushed his forces in a race for the Yalu River border with Chinese Manchuria. He promised his troops that they would be home for Christmas.

But fate, or perhaps just a blend of continued gross misjudgement of both civil and military intelligence and a general's impulsiveness, would determine a disastrous and humiliating outcome. For President Truman, this was the last straw. His relationship with MacArthur had become increasingly strained as the general continued to treat the establishment and Truman personally with disdain. On 11 April 1950, MacArthur was stripped of all his Far East commands.

Washington's miscalculations of China's intentions became rudely and painfully evident in late November when swarms of Chinese troops fell on the US I and IX Corps, while simultaneously jumping off from Tŏkch'ŏn to plough through the ROKA II Corps. The following two months witnessed the longest retreat in the history of the American military, as hundreds of thousands of largely illiterate, peasant soldiers steamrolled the UN forces back down the peninsula and beyond the 38th Parallel.

This was a different type of foe, striking at night in overwhelming numbers while blowing bugles and whistles and screaming as they attacked, unnerving many a South Korean soldier to the extent of precipitating widespread flight. The UN forces suffered successive costly defeats, such as at Chosin, Imjin and Kap'yŏng, and now faced being swept into the Sea of Japan.

Truman now publicly announced that the use of atomic bombs was under consideration to check the Red tide. The US Strategic Air Command was placed on alert for an immediate deployment of medium bombers to the Far East. Should they go, it would be with atomic capabilities, or what the Pentagon liked to refer to as 'weapons of mass destruction'. At this time, the Soviet nuclear arsenal was relatively small and that of Communist China non-existent.

As early as August Washington had kept open the option of the employment of nuclear assets in the Korean War. MacArthur, however, saw nuclear weapons as being of tactical value, targeting enemy lines of supply such as the rail network, including the destruction of tunnels. But the Pentagon did not believe that such an application would be practical, and would adhere to the exploitation of air supremacy.

The North Korean air capabilities were non-existent and Communist China was still building its own air force with help from the Soviet Union. The only significant threat to the Americans and her allies was MiG Alley, a zone restricted to the western stretches of the Yalu River because of limited flying time from bases in Manchuria. During the war, United Nations air forces flew more than one million sorties. This included the delivery of 476,000 tons of ordnance. Air interdiction, or deep air support, bombing was a strategy extensively employed by the US Air Force during the war, targeting industrial, transport and military centres well to the rear of the front. Over 15,000 interdiction sorties were conducted against North Korean targets, resulting in immense damage to North Korean cities and towns. It is estimated that 75 per cent of the North Korean capital P'yŏngyang was destroyed.

Since the war, much has changed, especially in the balance of power in the Far East. But some things have remained constant. Korea is as divided as ever, North and South separated by a chasm of ideological, political and economic differences, a polarity that defies any semblance of commonality.

South Korea, officially the Republic of Korea, has grown into an economic powerhouse to become the world's twelfth-largest economy. At 600,000 personnel, South Korea has one of the world's largest active armies, and with compulsory national conscription, has 3,100,000 reservists. The nation has a modern, sophisticated navy, with some of the most up-to-date equipment such as the American Aegis integrated naval weapons system. Vessels such as the Dokdo-class amphibious assault ship are built in South Korea. At 840 aircraft, South Korea boasts the world's ninth-largest air force, which includes the indigenous KAI T-50 Golden Eagle supersonic fighter. The United States maintains a military presence in South Korea of around 28,000 personnel of the US Eighth Army and the US Seventh Air Force. The United Nations Command is still in existence in South Korea.

In Japan, the United States Forces Japan (USFJ), with a strength of approximately 50,000 personnel, replaced the Far East Command in 1957. The port city of Yokosuka at the mouth of Tokyo Bay is home to US Seventh Fleet, which is made up of 60 to 70 ships, 300 aircraft and 40,000 naval and US Marines Corps personnel. Headquartered at Busan (formerly Pusan) Naval Base in South Korea, Commander, U.S. Naval Forces Korea, under the US Seventh Fleet command, is responsible for all US naval activities on the peninsula, including control of Chinhae, the only naval installation in South Korea.

North Korea remains in the absolute control of the Kim dynasty of dictators, with the state owning the means of production in a nationalized economy. International trade, including imports, is embargoed by the United States, leaving Communist China as North Korea's largest trading partner at 84 per cent of total external trade. The nation's economy, ranked 179th in the world, continues to struggle.

With an active army in excess of 1.1 million, North Korea has the fourth-largest military force in the world after China, the United States and India. It is estimated that around 20 per cent of males aged 17–54 are in North Korea's regular uniformed services. The military reserve is a massive 8.4 million. The nation's forces are very well equipped, including 3,700 tanks, 18,000 artillery pieces, 1,600 aircraft and 1,000 naval vessels. It has the world's largest fleet of submarines. The North Koreans possess nuclear capabilities, but the size and type of its arsenal is largely unknown. At 20 per cent of gross domestic product, North Korea's military expenditure is the highest in the world.

The People's Republic of China has, arising out of widespread reforms following the death of Mao Zedong in 1976, become one of the world's fastest-growing economies. By 2010, it had grown to be the world's second-largest economy. The People's Liberation

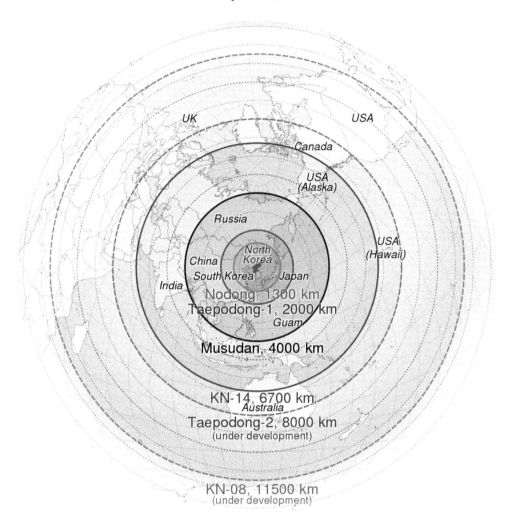

An azimuthal equidistant projection of estimated maximum range of some existing North Korean missiles in addition to those still being developed. (Image Cmglee)

Army strength of 2.3 million troops makes it the world's largest, with reserves second only to North Korea. Indigenous manufacture accounts for most of China's military requirements, particularly in the field of 5th-generation fighter aircraft from the Chengdu stable. The People's Liberation Army Navy has a strength of 255,000 personnel and 512 vessels, including 75 submarines.

China, second-smallest nuclear arsenal of the five nuclear-weapon states, has expanded its military capabilities to become a regional military power, and considered by many to have attained superpower status.

From Mao's proclamation of China as a communist people's republic in September 1949, the nation's military machinery has undergone a phenomenal transformation.

Combat success against Chiang Kai-shek's Nationalist army in 1948 and against United Nations forces in Korea was largely attributable to the sheer weight of expendable infantry that the Chinese threw at its opponents on the battlefield. Beijing's appeals to Stalin for the provision of air support for its military expedition into Korea fell on deaf ears, leaving the Chinese at a major disadvantage in battle when helpless to counter American air power. Communist China has ensured that its forces would never again find itself wanting in such a scenario.

Today, the stakes are much higher and the risk of a global nuclear conflagration considerably greater. Technological advances have made the tactics and strategies of the 1950s and 1960s obsolete. In the region, the same principal protagonists remain in uncomfortably close proximity to each other. Any new offensive would have to be without warning, brutally quick in employing maximum assets, and immediately and surgically decisive. There would be no second opportunity, as the retaliation would inevitably have the same objective: total annihilation in one swift blow.

However, troop concentrations and movements would not go unnoticed by the omnipresent spy satellites, high-altitude reconnaissance aircraft, drones and a miscellany of other 'listening' and surveillance devices and applications. Missile launches would most likely be preceded by a cyber-attack on the enemy's key electronic systems. It therefore makes sense that the United States and South Korea have established multi-layered Patriot/Cheolmae II missile systems near the demilitarized zone to intercept North Korean

Leader of the Democratic People's Republic of Korea (DPRK), Kim Jong-un (left), at an official reception hosted by Russian President Vladimir Putin, Vladivostok, Russian Island, 25 April, 2019. (Photo www.kremlin.ru)

short-range ballistic missiles. Some Patriot batteries have also been upgraded and equipped with PAC-2 and PAC-3 missiles designed to intercept incoming aircraft and missiles at altitudes of around 12–25 miles.

But who would be brave—or foolish—enough to execute the first strike?

Stalin kept the Korean War at arm's length, electing to use Kim Il-sung to do his bidding. There is no reason to believe that modern-day Russia harbours any expansionist plans on the Korean peninsula. If Moscow decided to flex its military muscle, it would be to reincorporate the Ukraine, and possibly the Baltic states and Belorussia into a Russia more akin to the days of the Soviet Union. In like manner, Communist China may want to fulfil its decades-old desire to force Taiwan into its fold.

Kim Il-sung's grandson, Kim Jong-un, became North Korea's third 'Supreme Leader' upon the death of his father, Kim Jong-il in 2011. Portrayed in state propaganda as a benevolent and revered marshal, Kim Jong-un is despotic in the methods he employs to stay in power for life, with fear being the preferred instrument.

At the 25th Session of the United Nations Human Rights Council convened on 7 February 2014, a report of the commission of inquiry on human rights in the Democratic People's Republic of Korea (document A/HRC/25/63) was tabled. Working in Seoul after having been refused access into North Korea, the commission found that

> systematic, widespread and gross human rights violations have been and are being committed by the Democratic People's Republic of Korea. In many instances, the violations found entailed crimes against humanity based on State policies. The main perpetrators are officials of the State Security Department, the Ministry of People's Security, the Korean People's Army, the Office of the Public Prosecutor, the judiciary and the Workers' Party of Korea, who are acting under the effective control of the central organs of the Workers' Party of Korea, the National Defence Commission and the Supreme Leader of the Democratic People's Republic of Korea.

In considering why such a situation would exist, the commission stressed that

> the current human rights situation in the Democratic People's Republic of Korea has been shaped by the historical experiences of the Korean people. Confucian social structures and the experience of the Japanese colonial occupation have to some degree informed the political structures and attitudes prevailing in the country today. The division imposed on the Korean peninsula, the massive destruction caused by the Korean War and the impact of the Cold War have engendered an isolationist mindset and an aversion to outside powers that are used to justify internal repression. The particular nature and the overall scale of human rights violations in the State can be more easily understood through an appreciation of the nature of its political system, which is based on a single party led by a single Supreme Leader, an elaborate guiding ideology and a centrally planned economy.

After the devastation of the Korean War suffered by the nation as a whole, particularly by its civilian population, its infrastructure and its towns, cities and villages, North Korea developed nuclear aspirations. In 1992, the International Atomic Energy Agency (IAEA) discovered that the country had understated its declaration of nuclear activities. Two years later, P'yŏngyang withdrew from the agency.

In a mission to prevent North Korea from also leaving the Nuclear Non-Proliferation Treaty (NPT), an agreement was entered into in which the United States would supply light-water reactors and energy assistance in return for North Korea halting its nuclear programme and allowing IAEA inspectors access to its facilities. By 2003 the agreement lay in tatters and P'yŏngyang unilaterally pulled out of the NPT.

The Six-Party talks ensued, in which China, Japan, Russia, South Korea and the United States employed diplomacy to dissuade North Korea from continuing with its nuclear activities. The negotiations failed and were called off in 2009.

Over the next few years tensions escalated in the region as North Korea increased its arsenal of ballistic missiles while developing more sophisticated models. In 2017, P'yŏngyang successfully test-fired its first intercontinental ballistic missiles (ICBMs), the Hwasong-14 (on 4 July) and Hwasong-15 (on 28 November), believed to have the capability of delivering a nuclear warhead anywhere in the United States.

Unexpectedly, but no doubt as a result of international sanctions against North Korea, in April 2018 Kim Jung-un announced a self-imposed moratorium on all testing of thermo-nuclear and ICBM weapons. Following each of the North Korean nuclear tests in 2006, 2009, 2013 and 2016, the United Nations Security Council passed a progressive tranche of resolutions imposing an ever-widening spectrum of sanctions.

With an apparent easing of tensions between the rogue state and the United States, and on the heels of a summit meeting between the leaders of North and South Korea, an historic meeting took place in Singapore on 12 June 2018 between US President Donald Trump and Kim Jong-un. Trump sought and received an undertaking from the North Korean leader to work towards a denuclearization of the Korean peninsula, but there was no binding agreement as Kim was not given an assurance that crippling sanctions would be lifted.

From 27/28 February 2019, the two leaders met again for another fruitless meeting, this time in Hanoi, Vietnam. Two months later, North Korea resumed the testing of short-range missiles for the first time in eighteen months, firing the road-mobile KN-23. Further tests were conducted in July and August. Submarine-based ballistic missiles were also tested and a space-launch vehicle, the Unha, also developed.

Most recently, Trump and Kim met at the DMZ on 30 June 2019, in what was little more than a photo-opportunity for Trump as he became the first sitting US president to set foot on North Korean soil. The dubious honeymoon, however, was short-lived. Clearly unhappy that consideration for the lifting of sanctions was wholly dependent on North Korea actively and visibly dismantling its nuclear programme, Kim threatened to unveil a new strategic weapon, announcing that he was binning his own moratorium on missile and nuclear tests.

US President Donald
J. Trump (left) greets North
Korean leader Kim Jong-un
for their second summit
meeting, Hanoi, Vietnam,
27 February, 2019. (Photo
Shealah Craighead,
White House)

Against a background of escalating anti-American public rhetoric fed through the
state-controlled media, North Korea continues to test-fire missiles into the Sea of Japan,
the 'target' itself regarded by Washington as a threat to Japan.

The legacy of the Korean War, including the causes and outcome, is as real today as the
1950–53 conflict itself. Only now, four potential protagonists face each other with sophisticated, destructive weaponry unimaginable back then. The enigma that is North Korea
has undergone a profound hardening of resolve, confident to the point of arrogance in
its newfound military prowess to openly defy and challenge the United States and her
South Korean protégé.

What has not remained a constant since the 1950s is the risk of a regional conflict
rapidly turning into an apocalyptic third world war. It is highly unlikely that either
Russia or Communist China would initiate a conflict in Korea—they have no reason to
do so, and must both be fully aware of the ramifications and repercussions of any such
direct act.

The United States, however, has a long history of becoming militarily involved in global hotspots going back to the early twentieth century: Panama, Cuba, Nicaragua, Vietnam, Afghanistan, Iraq, Libya, Somalia, Yugoslavia. Would the Trump administration conduct a limited pre-emptive strike against a perceived imminent threat from North Korea? Quite likely.

Is North Korea's sabre-rattling and hostile rhetoric merely designed to pressure the West into lifting sanctions? Possibly. Kim Jung-un, however, continues to show his total disregard for the fripperies of conventions, treaties, international law and meetings, so would North Korea suddenly launch missiles into South Korea? Perhaps more than just possibly.

President of South Korea, Moon Jae-in (right) embraces North Korean leader Kim Jong-un at the inter-Korean Summit, Peace House, in the Joint Security Area on the southern side of the Military Demarcation Line, 1 April 2018. (Photo Cheongwadae/Blue House)

BIBLIOGRAPHY

1st Marine Division Historical Diary – November 1950 (National Archives and Records Administration, College Park Maryland).

1st Marine Division Special Action Diary – October 1950–December 1950 (National Archives and Records Administration, College Park Maryland).

27th British Commonwealth Brigade War Diary September to November 1950 (The Australia War Memorial archives, Campbell).

3rd Battalion, The Royal Australian War Diary November 1950 (The Australia War Memorial archives, Campbell).

Boose, Donald W. Jnr, *US Army Forces in the Korean War* (Osprey Publishing, Oxford, 2005).

Central Intelligence Agency (CIA) declassified documents.

Cunningham-Boothe, Ashley and Peter Farrar, Eds., *British Forces in the Korean War* (British Korean Veterans Association, 1997).

Fehrenbach, T.R., *This Kind of War: The Classic Korean War History* (Potomac Books, 2000).

Futrell, Robert Frank, *The United States Air Force in Korea, 1950–1953* (Progressive Management, 1983).

Gugeler, Russell A., *Combat Actions in Korea* (Center of Military History, United States Army, Washington D.C., 1954).

Hastings, Max, *The Korean War* (Pan, London, 1987).

Korean War Project, www.koreanwar.org/

Latham, William Clark, *Cold Days in Hell: American POWs in Korea* (Texas A&M University Press, 2013).

MacKenzie, S.P., *The Imjin and Kapyong Battle, Korea, 1951* (Indiana University Press, Bloomington, 2013).

Mao, Min, *Marshal Peng De-huai* (2018).

McGovern, James, *To the Yalu: From the Chinese Invasion of Korea to MacArthur's Dismissal* (William Morrow, New York, 1972).

Montross, L., et al, *U.S. Marine Operations in Korea, 1950–1953* (US Government Printing Office, Washington, 1962).

Mossman, Billy C., *Ebb and Flow, November 1950–July 1951* (Center of Military History, United States Army, Washington, 1990).

Rees, David, *Korea: The Limited War* (Pelican Books, Baltimore, 1970).

Tucker, Spencer C., Ed., *Encyclopedia of the Korean War* (Checkmark Books, New York, 2002).

United Nations Command, Military Intelligence Section, *Korea, A Summary 25 June 1950–25 April 1952.*

United States Army Records, National Archives and Records Administration (NARA), College Park, Maryland, USA.

US Navy, US Marine Corps and Coast Guard historical offices, *The Sea Services in the Korean War, 1950–1953* (US Naval Institute, Annapolis, 1957, 2000)

van Tonder, Gerry, *North Korea Invades the South: Across the 38th Parallel, June 1950* (Pen and Sword Military, Barnsley, 2018)

van Tonder, Gerry, *North Korean Onslaught: UN Stand at the Pusan Perimeter, August–September 1950* (Pen and Sword Military, Barnsley, 2018)

van Tonder, Gerry, *Korean War, Inchon Landing: MacArthur's Masterstroke, September 1950* (Pen and Sword Military, Barnsley, 2019)

van Tonder, Gerry, *Korean War Allied Surge: Pyongyang Falls, UN Sweep to the Yalu, October 1950* (Pen and Sword Military, Barnsley, 2019).

van Tonder, Gerry, *Korean War: Chinese Invasion: People's Liberation Army Crosses the Yalu October 1950—March 1951* (Pen and Sword Military, Barnsley, 2019).

War Diary X Corps Monthly Summary 1 Oct 1950 to 31 Oct 1950.

Weintraub, Stanley, *A Christmas Far from Home: An Epic Tale of Courage and Survival during the Korean War* (Hachette, UK, 2014).

Watson, Brent (2000) 'Recipe for Victory: The Fight for Hill 677 during the Battle of the Kap'yong River, 24–25 April 1951' in *Canadian Military History*: Vol. 9: Issue 2, Article 2.

Whiting, Allen S., *China Crosses the Yalu, The Decision to Enter the Korean War* (Stanford University Press, Stanford, 1968).

Xiaoming Zhang, *Red Wings Over the Yalu* (Texas A&M University Press, 2002).

Index

Rickord, Maj Gerald 29
Ridgway, Lt Gen Matthew B. 14,
  17, 24, 69-71, 82, 84-85
ROKA *see* Republic of Korea
  Army (South Korean)
Ross, Lt H. 62
Royal Australian Air Force 93
Ruffner, Maj Gen Clark L. 14, 73,
  76, 96
Ruiz-Novoa, Lt Col Alberto 98
Rusk, Dean 58
Russell, Lt Walter B. 99

Saamch'ŏn 93
Samich'ŏn 91, 100, 106, 108
Samyang-ni 79
Sariwŏn 12
Sat'ae-ri Valley 86-90
Seoul 10-11, 16-18, 25, 48, 66-67,
  69-70, 77, 90, 91, 100, 119
Sinanju 31, 93
Smith, Capt Claude 47
Smith, Lt Col Charles B. 10
Smith, Lt Gormon C. 100
Smith, Maj Gen Oliver P. 14, 97
Smooth, Gen 33
Solma-ri 30, 37, 39, 43, 50
Soule, Maj Gen Robert H. 25, 34,
  41-43, 45-46, 91
South African Air Force 93
Soyang River 67, 72
Speakman, Pte William
  104-105
Spence, Maj James 110
Stalin, Joseph 9, 113, 118-119
Stone, Lt-Col James R. 58-60, 64
Stratemeyer, Gen George E.
  75-76
Sunch'ŏn 93
Suwŏn 10
Swift, Maj Gen Ira P. 91

T'aech'ŏn 92-93
Taebaek Mountains 25
Taegu 11, 31
Taejŏn 10, 31
Taylor, Brig George 53, 65
Taylor, Lt Gen Maxwell 98
Temple, Lt Guy 27-28
Tŏkch'ŏn 12, 115
Tokyo 9, 24, 70, 86, 113-114, 116
Triangle Hill
Trudeau, Lt-Col Louis 103
Trudeau, Maj Gen Arthur G. 99
Truell, Lt George 29
Truman, Harry S. 9, 12, 19-20,
  22-24, 35, 115

Turkish Brigade (UNC) 34, 69,
  80, 110
Turner Joy, V Adm C. 83

Ŭijŏngbu 17, 46, 67-69, 71, 79
United Nations (UN) 9-10, 22,
  25-26, 35, 61, 82, 111, 113-114,
  119-120
United Nations Command
  (UNC) *also* forces 10-12, 14,
  16-19, 24-26, 30, 45, 58, 66,
  68-71, 77-78, 80-82, 84-85,
  88-98, 103, 109-110, 113-116, 118
United States Atomic Energy
  Commission 20
US Air Force 31, 36, 48, 75, 93, 96
  Far East Air Force (FEAF)
    31-32, 73, 75, 79, 81, 92-94
  Bomber Command 92
  Fifth Air Force 90, 95-96
  Seventh Air Force 116
  3rd Bombardment Group
    78, 80
  8th Operations Group 32
  9th Bombardment Wing 22
  19th Bombardment Group
    80, 93
  98th Bombardment Wing
    80, 93
  307th Bombardment Wing
    80, 93
  452nd Bombardment Wing 31
  502nd Tactical Air Control
    Group 31
  6147th Tactical Air Control
    Group 78
US Army 45, 64, 69, 110
  Eighth Army 10-12, 14, 16-18,
    24-25, 31-32, 43, 65-66,
    70-71, 75, 79, 86, 90, 98,
    113, 116
  by corps
    I Corps 16-18, 25, 33, 39,
      43, 45-46, 54, 67-69, 77,
      79-80, 91-92, 96, 100, 103,
      106-107, 114
    IX Corps 15-18, 26, 33, 54,
      56, 59, 67, 72, 75, 77,
      79-80, 91, 96, 98
    X Corps 11-12, 67, 71-73,
      75-77, 80, 85, 88, 100, 114
  by division
    1st Cavalry Division 10, 12,
      14, 16, 61, 80, 91-92
    2nd Infantry Division 11,
      14, 67, 71, 73, 75-77, 80,
      85-86, 88, 90, 98

3rd Infantry Division
  16, 17-18, 25-26, 34, 42,
  45-46, 68, 75, 80, 85, 91
7th Infantry Division 11,
  14, 43, 67, 75, 80, 97-100
24th Infantry Division 10,
  14, 16-17, 25, 33-34, 46,
  54, 56, 67-68
25th Infantry Division 10,
  14, 16-17, 25-26, 34, 46,
  68-69, 80, 91
40th Infantry Division 80
45th Infantry Division 92,
  96, 103
US Far East Command 10, 116
US Marine Corps 11, 16, 67, 81,
  100-103, 107-110, 116
  1st Marine Air Wing 102
    Marine Attack Squadron
    311 (VMA-311) 101
  1st Marine Division 11, 14, 16,
    33, 54, 67, 71, 75, 80, 100,
    103, 107
US Navy 101, 116
  Seventh Fleet 116
  USS *Toledo* 69
US Strategic Air Command 12,
  21, 115

Van Fleet, Gen James A. 24-25,
  43, 51, 66-67, 69-72, 75, 77-79,
  86, 97, 98
Vernerrey, Lt Col Magrin 77

Wake Island conference 12,
  19-20, 23
Walker, Lt Gen Walton H. 10-12,
  14, 113-114
Weyand, Lt Col Fred C. 35
Weyland, Gen Otto P. 93
White Horse 71, 96-97
Williams, Maj George H. 88
Wilton, Brig John 107
Wisbey, Capt Frank 44
Wŏnju 17
Wŏnsan 12, 25, 82
Woods, Lt Col John O. 88

Yalu River 11-12, 17, 22, 115
Yanggu 67
Yangyang 67, 78-79
Yŏnch'ŏn 80, 90
Yŏngwŏn 12
Young, Maj Gen Robert N. 88
Younger, Maj Anthony 45
Yu Jae Hung, Gen 14

About the Author

Born in Southern Rhodesia, now Zimbabwe, historian and author Gerry van Tonder came to Britain in 1999. Specializing in military history, Gerry started his writing career with titles about twentieth-century guerrilla and open warfare in southern Africa, including the co-authored definitive *Rhodesia Regiment 1899–1981*. Gerry presented a copy of this title to the regiment's former colonel-in-chief, Her Majesty the Queen. Having written over twenty books, Gerry writes extensively for several Pen & Sword military history series including 'Cold War 1945–1991', 'Military Legacy' (focusing on the heritage of British cities), 'Echoes of the Blitz', and 'History of Terror'.

Other titles by Gerry van Tonder

Berlin Blockade: Soviet Chokehold and the Great Allied Airlift 1948–1949
Chesterfield's Military Heritage
Derby in 50 Buildings
Echoes of the Coventry Blitz
Irgun: Revisionist Zionism 1931–1948
North Korea Invades the South: Across the 38th Parallel, June 1950
North Korean Onslaught: UN Stand at the Pusan Perimeter, August–September 1950
Korean War: Inchon Landing: MacArthur's Masterstroke, September 1950
Korean War: Allied Surge: Pyongyang Falls, UN Sweep to the Yalu, October 1950
Korean War: Chinese Invasion: People's Liberation Army Crosses the Yalu October 1950—March 1951
Lt-Gen Keith Coster: A Life in Uniform
Malayan Emergency: Triumph of the Running Dogs 1948–1960
Mansfield Through Time
North of the Red Line: Recollections of the Border War by Members of the South African Armed Forces: 1966–1989
Nottingham's Military Legacy
Operation Lighthouse: Intaf in the Rhodesian Bush War 1972–1980
Red China: Mao Crushes Chiang's Kuomintang, 1949
Rhodesia Regiment 1899–1981
Rhodesian African Rifles/Rhodesia Native Regiment Book of Remembrance
Rhodesian Combined Forces Roll of Honour 1966-1981
Sheffield's Military Legacy
Sino-Indian War: October–November 1962
SS Einsatzgruppen: Nazi Death Squads 1939–1945